"50 Ways To Make Money With GPT"

Introduction

In the ever-evolving digital age, artificial intelligence has become a powerful tool, transforming industries and creating new opportunities. One of the most revolutionary advancements in AI is the rise of Generative Pretrained Transformers (GPT). This cutting-edge technology, known for its ability to generate human-like text, has opened doors for innovative ways to earn an income. "50 Ways To Make Money With GPT" is your gateway to exploring these opportunities.

Whether you're a freelancer, business owner, or someone looking for a new stream of income, GPT can offer versatile and profitable solutions. From generating content to automating tasks, GPT's capabilities can save time and enhance productivity, allowing you to focus on what matters most—growing your income. This eBook presents fifty different methods, each tailored to help you monetise GPT's unique abilities in practical, creative, and scalable ways.

The beauty of GPT lies in its flexibility. You can use it to generate blog posts, write compelling product descriptions, create marketing copy, assist with coding, and even develop personalised tutoring services. No matter your level of experience with AI, this guide provides clear, actionable ideas that can be implemented immediately.

Throughout the chapters, we'll cover diverse avenues for earning money, ranging from traditional freelancing opportunities to more innovative uses of GPT, like AI-driven business models and automation services. Each section includes practical tips, examples, and resources to help you maximise your earning potential. With AI technology advancing at a rapid pace, now is the perfect time to capitalise on these opportunities. "50 Ways To Make Money With GPT" will show you how to leverage the power of AI to enhance your skill set, boost your productivity, and ultimately, increase your income.

Index

10. Ghostwriting Services
11. Writing Newsletters
12. AI-Powered Script Writing for Videos
13. Website Content Generation
14. Writing E-books for Passive Income
15. Proofreading and Editing Services
16. Translating Text Using GPT
17. Summarising Academic Papers
18. Creating AI-Generated Poetry
19. Personalised Resume and Cover Letter Writing
20. Developing Business Plans
21. Writing White Papers and Reports
22. Generating Customer Support Responses
23. Automated Chatbot Creation
24. Offering AI-Powered Tutoring Services
25. Developing Personalised Learning Plans
26. Assisting with Research and Data Analysis
27. AI-Powered Writing Assistant Tools
28. Customised Social Media Captions
29. Writing Reviews and Testimonials
30. Creating AI-Driven Product Suggestions
31. Providing AI Content Consulting
32. Creating AI-Powered Websites or Blogs
33. Automating Business Workflows with GPT
34. Generating Stock Market Analysis Reports
35. Producing AI-Powered Financial Newsletters
36. Offering Custom AI Chatbot Development
37. Building Niche Affiliate Marketing Websites
38. Developing AI-Generated Fiction Stories

Chapter 1
Freelance Writing with GPT

Freelance writing has long been a lucrative way to earn money online, and with the advent of GPT technology, it has become even more accessible. GPT can assist writers by generating content quickly, improving productivity, and enhancing creativity. This chapter will guide you through using GPT effectively in freelance writing, offering practical tips, examples, and resources to maximise your earning potential.

How GPT Can Assist Freelance Writers

GPT can help streamline the writing process by generating high-quality text on a variety of topics. As a freelance writer, you can use GPT to:

- **Draft content quickly** : GPT can create first drafts of articles, blog posts, or other written material, which you can then refine.
- **Overcome writer's block** : If you struggle to start a piece, GPT can provide ideas and outlines to get you going.
- **Produce SEO-friendly content** : GPT can help generate keyword-optimised content for search engine rankings, saving time on research.
- **Diversify writing styles** : With GPT, you can adapt your tone and style to suit different clients, from formal reports to conversational blog posts.

Practical Tips to Maximise Earnings

1. **Choose high-demand niches** : Focus on industries such as technology, healthcare, finance, or e-commerce, where well-

researched and SEO-optimised content is highly valued.

2. **Use GPT as an assistant, not a replacement** : GPT can provide a foundation for your writing, but human refinement is key to quality. Always personalise the content to suit your client's needs.

3. **Offer value-added services** : Expand your offerings by including SEO analysis, keyword research, and proofreading services alongside content writing.

4. **Build a portfolio** : Showcase your ability to use AI tools effectively by creating a portfolio of GPT-enhanced writing samples, highlighting how the technology helps you meet clients' objectives faster and more efficiently.

Example: Blog Post Generation

Let's say a client requests a blog post on the latest trends in digital marketing. Using GPT, you can input the topic and get a detailed outline or a draft with key points. You can then review and refine the content, adding a human touch to ensure the article is accurate and engaging. The ability to generate content quickly allows you to take on more projects, increasing your overall earnings.

Resources to Enhance Your Freelance Writing with GPT

- **OpenAI's GPT-4 API** : This is the most advanced version of GPT, offering versatile options for text generation.
- **SEO Tools** : Platforms like SEMrush or Ahrefs can help you optimise GPT-generated content with relevant keywords for better visibility.
- **Writing Platforms** : Websites like Upwork, Fiverr, and Freelancer allow you to offer freelance writing services, making it easy to find clients in need of quick, quality content.

By incorporating GPT into your freelance writing workflow, you can increase efficiency, reduce turnaround times, and deliver high-quality content consistently. This will enable you to take on more projects, enhance your reputation, and ultimately boost your income.

Chapter 2
Blog Post Generation

Blog post generation is one of the most popular ways to leverage GPT for earning money. Whether you're a freelancer, business owner, or content creator, GPT can help you produce high-quality blog content quickly and efficiently. This chapter will guide you through using GPT for blog post generation, offering practical tips, examples, and resources to help you maximise your earning potential.

How GPT Can Help with Blog Post Generation

GPT can significantly streamline the process of writing blog posts by:

- **Generating topic ideas** : Based on your niche or target audience, GPT can suggest relevant and trending blog post topics.
- **Creating detailed outlines** : It can provide structured outlines, including headings, subheadings, and key points to cover.
- **Writing content** : GPT can produce the first draft of your blog post, making it easier to edit and refine.
- **Improving SEO** : By integrating keywords into the content naturally, GPT can assist in

creating SEO-friendly blog posts that rank well on search engines.

Practical Tips to Maximise Earnings

1. **Focus on profitable niches** : Write blog posts in high-demand areas such as technology, finance, health, or e-commerce. These industries often pay well for informative, optimised content.
2. **Enhance SEO** : While GPT can help with SEO, you should still use tools like SEMrush or Ahrefs to refine keyword placement and ensure the content meets current SEO standards.
3. **Personalise and refine** : Always review GPT-generated content and tailor it to the client's style and voice. This will help you deliver unique, high-quality work that stands out.
4. **Offer bulk content packages** : Many clients need regular blog posts. Offering bulk packages or monthly subscriptions can help you secure recurring income and build long-term client relationships.
5. **Add value with visuals** : Consider offering image sourcing or the creation of

infographics alongside the blog posts to add value for your clients.

Example: Generating a Blog Post on Sustainable Living

Let's say a client requests a blog post on "How to Live Sustainably in 2024." You can start by asking GPT for an outline, which may include sections such as "Why Sustainable Living Matters," "Practical Steps for Sustainable Living," and "The Future of Sustainability." Once the outline is generated, GPT can provide draft content for each section. You can then edit and refine the language, ensuring it aligns with the client's voice and values. This process allows you to complete a high-quality blog post much faster than writing it from scratch.

Resources to Boost Your Blog Post Generation Business

- **OpenAI's GPT-4 API** : This powerful AI tool can generate high-quality content quickly, helping you meet tight deadlines.

- **SEO Platforms** : Use tools like Yoast, Moz, or SEMrush to optimise GPT-generated content for search engines.
- **Content Management Systems** : Platforms like WordPress, Wix, or Squarespace can help you build a blog or offer blog post services to clients directly.
- **Freelance Marketplaces** : Websites like Upwork, Fiverr, and Freelancer can help you find clients looking for blog post writers.

By incorporating GPT into your blog post generation process, you can take on more projects, reduce your workload, and ensure faster delivery times. With the right SEO optimisation and personalisation, you can offer valuable, scalable content creation services that boost your income while satisfying your clients' needs.

Chapter 3
SEO-Optimised Content Creation

SEO-optimised content creation is a crucial service for businesses looking to rank higher on search engines and attract more traffic to their websites. By using GPT technology, you can streamline the process of creating keyword-rich, relevant content that meets both client and search engine requirements. This chapter outlines how

GPT can be used to generate SEO-friendly content, offering practical tips, examples, and resources to maximise your earning potential.

How GPT Can Help with SEO-Optimised Content Creation

GPT is a powerful tool that can assist with:

- **Keyword integration** : GPT can generate content that naturally incorporates important keywords, making it easier for the content to rank higher in search results.
- **Meta descriptions and tags** : It can help you craft compelling meta descriptions and tags, essential for SEO.
- **Content structuring** : GPT can format content into SEO-friendly structures, such as using headings (H1, H2, H3), lists, and bullet points, all of which are preferred by search engines.
- **Long-form content** : GPT can help create detailed and informative articles, which tend to perform better in search engine rankings.

Practical Tips to Maximise Earnings

1. **Research keywords** : Before using GPT, conduct thorough keyword research using tools like Google Keyword Planner, Ahrefs, or SEMrush. Provide these keywords to GPT to ensure the content it generates is fully optimised for search engines.
2. **Focus on long-tail keywords** : Long-tail keywords are more specific and less competitive, making it easier for content to rank. Use GPT to write content that targets these niche search terms.
3. **Optimise readability** : Ensure GPT-generated content is easy to read by breaking it into short paragraphs, using bullet points, and adding clear headings and subheadings. Content that is readable tends to perform better in search rankings.
4. **Use LSI (Latent Semantic Indexing) keywords** : In addition to the primary keywords, ask GPT to include related terms or synonyms, improving the content's relevance and searchability.
5. **Add internal and external links** : GPT can help suggest logical points to insert links to other pages on the client's website (internal links) and reputable external sources, both of which boost SEO performance.

Example: SEO-Optimised Blog Post on Vegan Recipes

Suppose a client asks for an SEO-optimised blog post on "Easy Vegan Recipes for Beginners" to drive traffic to their food blog. You can start by researching relevant keywords such as "vegan recipes," "easy vegan meals," and "plant-based beginner recipes" using an SEO tool. Provide GPT with these keywords and ask it to generate an article with sections like "Top 5 Easy Vegan Recipes" or "How to Get Started with Vegan Cooking."

GPT can then create a structured blog post that includes headings (e.g. H2 for the recipe categories), naturally integrates keywords, and maintains a conversational tone that appeals to the target audience. Once the content is generated, you can tweak it to ensure it aligns with the client's voice and includes the necessary internal and external links.

Resources to Boost Your SEO-Optimised Content Creation Business

- **SEO Tools** : Tools like SEMrush, Moz, Ahrefs, and Google Keyword Planner are essential for conducting thorough keyword research and tracking performance.

- **GPT Integration** : OpenAI's GPT-4 API is a powerful tool for generating SEO-friendly content quickly and efficiently.
- **SEO Plugins** : If you're managing a client's blog on WordPress, use SEO plugins like Yoast SEO or All in One SEO to ensure the content is fully optimised.
- **Content Analysis Tools** : Use tools like Hemingway or Grammarly to improve readability and ensure your content is polished before submitting it to clients.

Maximising Earnings with SEO Content

1. **Offer specialised SEO services** : Beyond just writing content, offer keyword research, on-page SEO optimisation, and SEO audits as part of your services.
2. **Charge for long-form content** : Clients often pay more for comprehensive, detailed blog posts or articles that can rank better on search engines.
3. **Work with high-demand industries** : Focus on industries like e-commerce, tech, health, and finance, where SEO is crucial for online visibility.

By mastering the art of SEO-optimised content creation using GPT, you can offer in-demand services that help clients rank higher on search engines, attract more visitors, and ultimately, boost their online presence. This will not only make your work more valuable but also enable you to command higher fees for your expertise.

Chapter 4
Copywriting for Advertisements

Copywriting for advertisements is one of the most lucrative applications of GPT technology, offering businesses the chance to craft persuasive, engaging, and impactful messages that convert audiences into customers. Whether you're working with large companies or small start-ups, GPT can assist in generating compelling ad copy that resonates with target audiences. This chapter will guide you through using GPT for advertisement copywriting, providing practical tips, examples, and resources to help you maximise your earning potential.

How GPT Can Assist in Copywriting for Advertisements

GPT can help in various stages of ad copy creation, including:

- **Headline generation** : Crafting catchy and attention-grabbing headlines to draw in readers or viewers.
- **Creating compelling body copy** : Generating persuasive, succinct, and benefit-focused content that conveys the product's value.
- **A/B testing variations** : Producing multiple versions of the same ad copy for testing which performs best in terms of click-through rates or conversions.
- **Tailoring content to platforms** : GPT can generate ad copy specific to platforms like Google Ads, Facebook, Instagram, LinkedIn, and email campaigns, ensuring it fits the format and audience of each platform.

Practical Tips to Maximise Earnings

1. **Understand your audience** : Before using GPT, define the target audience's needs, preferences, and pain points. You can then instruct GPT to focus on messaging that speaks directly to these aspects, making the ad more impactful.
2. **Use the AIDA formula** : GPT can generate content following the AIDA (Attention, Interest, Desire, Action) structure, ensuring the copy engages the reader at every stage. Ask GPT to prioritise this structure in its outputs.
3. **Focus on benefits over features** : Ensure the copy emphasises how a product or service benefits the user, rather than listing features. For instance, instead of saying, "This vacuum has a HEPA filter," you'd say, "Breathe easier with a vacuum that removes 99% of allergens."
4. **Optimise for specific platforms** : Tailor the GPT-generated copy for specific advertising platforms. For example, use concise, catchy lines for Google Ads, and more detailed, engaging content for social media platforms like Facebook.
5. **Offer A/B testing variations** : As part of your service, use GPT to create multiple ad

variations for A/B testing, helping your clients determine which version performs best.

Example: Creating a Facebook Ad for a Fitness App

Let's say a client wants a Facebook ad for their new fitness app. You can instruct GPT to generate an attention-grabbing headline such as, "Get Fit from Home in Just 15 Minutes a Day!" For the body copy, GPT might write something like, "Join our fitness app and access hundreds of quick, effective workouts designed to fit into your busy schedule. No equipment needed, just your determination. Start your free trial today!" This copy is concise, highlights the benefits, and includes a clear call to action, which is essential for ad success.
You can also ask GPT to create multiple versions of the ad by changing the headline and key points, providing the client with options to test which resonates most with their audience.

Resources to Boost Your Copywriting for Advertisements Business

- **Ad Copy Tools** : Platforms like Google Ads, Facebook Ads Manager, and LinkedIn Ads provide templates and insights on ad formats, helping you customise GPT-generated copy to fit each platform's requirements.
- **Copywriting Frameworks** : Familiarise yourself with established copywriting formulas such as AIDA (Attention, Interest, Desire, Action) and PAS (Problem, Agitate, Solution) to enhance GPT outputs.
- **GPT Tools** : Use OpenAI's GPT-4 API to generate ad copy quickly, allowing you to work on multiple projects simultaneously without compromising quality.
- **Ad Performance Tracking** : Tools like Google Analytics and Facebook Pixel can help you monitor the performance of your ads and adjust copy accordingly for better conversions.

Maximising Earnings with Copywriting

1. **Expand your services** : Offer comprehensive packages that include not only ad copywriting but also A/B testing, keyword optimisation for Google Ads, and performance monitoring.
2. **Target high-demand sectors** : Focus on industries that heavily invest in digital advertising, such as e-commerce, tech, real estate, and healthcare. These sectors often require frequent ad copy updates and are willing to pay a premium for effective content.
3. **Charge by platform** : Since different platforms require varied copy styles, consider charging per platform (e.g., separate rates for Google Ads, Facebook Ads, Instagram) or by the number of variations created for A/B testing.

By leveraging GPT for copywriting, you can produce high-quality advertisements faster, serve a wider range of clients, and offer a service that directly impacts your clients' sales and conversions. This not only helps you meet client expectations but also allows you to command higher rates and increase your earning potential.

Chapter 5
Social Media Content Creation

Social media content creation is an essential service for businesses and influencers looking to engage with their audience and grow their online presence. With GPT technology, generating engaging and relevant social media posts has become easier and faster. This chapter explores how to use GPT for social media content creation, offering practical tips, examples, and resources to help you maximise your earning potential.

How GPT Can Assist in Social Media Content Creation

GPT can be a valuable tool for creating a wide variety of social media content, such as:

- **Short-form posts** : Generate concise, attention-grabbing content for platforms like Twitter, Instagram, and LinkedIn.
- **Captions for images** : Write creative and engaging captions for photos or graphics to boost interaction and engagement.

- **Hashtag suggestions** : GPT can recommend relevant hashtags based on the post's content and the target audience.
- **Content calendars** : Generate ideas for a month's worth of posts, helping you or your clients maintain a consistent online presence.
- **Ad copy for social platforms** : Create compelling ads tailored to platforms like Facebook, Instagram, or LinkedIn that align with the brand's tone and objectives.

Practical Tips to Maximise Earnings

1. **Understand the platform's tone and format** : GPT-generated content must be tailored to each platform's unique style. For example, Instagram posts might require a more visual, casual tone, while LinkedIn posts might need a professional, thought-leadership approach. Instruct GPT accordingly.
2. **Use relevant hashtags** : Social media algorithms favour posts with effective hashtag use. GPT can generate hashtag suggestions, but you should always research current trends and popular

hashtags in your niche to maximise post visibility.

3. **Engage with trending topics** : Ask GPT to generate content that taps into current trends, viral challenges, or seasonal events. This will help increase visibility and engagement, making the content more shareable.

4. **Keep posts short and engaging** : Social media audiences have short attention spans. Use GPT to generate snappy, creative content that gets to the point quickly while encouraging likes, shares, and comments.

5. **Create content calendars** : Offer clients a full content calendar service, where you use GPT to generate a month's worth of posts in advance. This ensures consistent posting, which is key for growing an online presence.

Example: Instagram Post for a Fashion Brand

Imagine you're tasked with creating an Instagram post for a fashion brand promoting a summer sale. You could ask GPT to generate a fun, engaging caption like, "☀□ Summer is here, and so are the savings! □ Get 30% off our hottest styles. Shop now and slay all season long □

#SummerSale #FashionDeals." You can then refine the caption to match the brand's tone, ensuring it resonates with the audience.
GPT can also suggest relevant hashtags such as #SummerStyle, #OOTD (Outfit of the Day), or #FashionInspo, helping the post reach a wider audience. You could offer variations for testing or create a content calendar with additional promotional posts over the course of the sale.

Resources to Boost Your Social Media Content Creation Business

- **Social Media Tools** : Tools like Hootsuite, Buffer, or Later can help schedule and manage posts across multiple platforms, increasing your efficiency.
- **Hashtag Research Tools** : Platforms like Hashtagify or All Hashtag can provide insights into trending and relevant hashtags, ensuring GPT's content is optimised for visibility.
- **GPT Integration** : Use OpenAI's GPT-4 API to quickly generate content ideas, captions, and posts for multiple social platforms.
- **Analytics Platforms** : Tools like Sprout Social or Google Analytics can help you track the performance of your posts,

allowing you to adjust content strategies based on data.

Maximising Earnings with Social Media Content Creation

1. **Offer multi-platform packages** : Provide packages where you create and manage content across multiple platforms (e.g., Instagram, Twitter, Facebook, LinkedIn). Clients appreciate a cohesive strategy across all channels.
2. **Create content calendars** : Many businesses struggle with maintaining consistency. By offering a monthly or weekly content calendar service, you can provide regular, consistent posts and charge a premium for this convenience.
3. **Engage in community management** : In addition to content creation, offer community management services such as responding to comments and messages, which adds value for clients and increases your earning potential.
4. **Monetise influencer collaborations** : Offer to create influencer-specific content, which helps brands craft messages that align with influencers' styles and audience

preferences, increasing the chances of successful collaborations.

By incorporating GPT into your social media content creation process, you can offer fast, engaging, and consistent content across platforms. This will enable you to take on more clients, boost their social media engagement, and enhance your earning potential with high-value services like content calendars and multi-platform management.

Chapter 6
Crafting Email Marketing Campaigns

Email marketing remains one of the most effective ways to engage with customers, drive conversions, and build long-term relationships. GPT can significantly enhance your ability to create persuasive, personalised, and engaging email marketing campaigns that convert readers into loyal customers. This chapter will provide practical tips, examples, and resources to help you maximise your earning potential when crafting email marketing campaigns using GPT.

How GPT Can Assist in Email Marketing Campaigns

GPT can streamline many aspects of email marketing, including:

- **Subject lines** : Crafting attention-grabbing and concise subject lines that increase open rates.
- **Personalised content** : Generating tailored email copy based on customer data, ensuring relevance and personal connection.
- **Call-to-action (CTA)** : Writing effective and clear CTAs that prompt recipients to take the desired action, such as clicking a link, making a purchase, or signing up for a service.
- **Drip campaigns** : Creating sequences of emails that nurture leads over time, offering value and building trust to guide them toward conversion.
- **Segmentation-specific emails** : Crafting tailored messages for different customer segments (e.g., new customers, repeat buyers, or abandoned cart emails).

Practical Tips to Maximise Earnings

1. **Write compelling subject lines** : GPT can suggest a range of subject lines, but make sure to test and refine these. Subject lines should be short, engaging, and create a sense of urgency or curiosity to increase open rates. For example, a subject like "Don't Miss Out: 50% Off Ends Today!" could perform well for a promotional campaign.

2. **Personalise your content** : Leverage customer data to ask GPT for personalised content. Include names, past purchase history, or recommendations based on behaviour to make the emails feel more relevant to each recipient.

3. **Optimise for mobile** : Ensure the content GPT generates is mobile-friendly, as many customers will read emails on their smartphones. Use clear, concise text, short paragraphs, and include a strong CTA that stands out.

4. **Focus on conversion** : Every email should have a clear goal, whether it's to drive sales, increase sign-ups, or promote a new product. GPT can help craft persuasive copy with a strong CTA, but make sure to test

variations to see what resonates with your audience.

5. **Test and analyse** : Use A/B testing to experiment with different subject lines, body copy, and CTAs. GPT can quickly generate variations, allowing you to find the most effective messaging.

Example: Promotional Email for an Online Store

Imagine a client asks for a promotional email to announce a seasonal sale. GPT can generate a subject line like "Summer Sale – Up to 40% Off Your Favourite Styles!" The body copy might start with a greeting, followed by a brief introduction: "Dear [Customer Name], Summer is here, and so are the savings! Shop our exclusive collection and enjoy up to 40% off on selected items. Hurry, the sale ends soon!"

The email can then include a CTA like, "Shop Now," linked to the online store, and close with a sense of urgency: "Don't miss out—get your favourites before they're gone!" Using GPT, you can create multiple variations of this email, optimising for different customer segments or products.

Resources to Boost Your Email Marketing Campaigns

- **Email Marketing Platforms** : Tools like Mailchimp, Constant Contact, and HubSpot allow you to design, send, and track email campaigns. GPT can help generate content quickly, which can then be integrated into these platforms.
- **A/B Testing Tools** : Platforms like Optimizely or VWO can help you test different email variations and track which performs best in terms of open rates and conversions.
- **Email Templates** : Websites like Litmus or Stripo offer ready-to-use email templates that you can combine with GPT-generated content to create professional and effective emails.
- **Analytics Tools** : Use email tracking tools from your email marketing platform to monitor open rates, click-through rates, and conversions. These insights will help refine your content strategy over time.

Maximising Earnings with Email Marketing Campaigns

1. **Offer comprehensive email marketing packages** : Go beyond writing a single email by offering entire campaigns, including promotional, welcome, nurture, and abandoned cart emails. Clients are often willing to pay more for complete campaign management.
2. **Charge per campaign or on retainer** : Clients often require ongoing email campaigns. Offer retainer services where you manage and craft regular emails over the long term, ensuring a consistent income.
3. **Target e-commerce and service-based businesses** : These businesses often rely heavily on email marketing for customer engagement and sales, making them ideal clients for email marketing services.
4. **Provide analytics and reporting** : Include performance tracking and analysis as part of your service, showing clients the ROI of the emails. This will add value to your offerings and justify premium pricing.

By integrating GPT into your email marketing campaigns, you can offer fast, efficient, and high-quality email copy that helps clients boost engagement and conversions. Combining this technology with best practices in personalisation, segmentation, and testing will allow you to create campaigns that not only deliver results but also maximise your earning potential.

Chapter 7
Writing Product Descriptions for E-commerce

Writing compelling product descriptions for e-commerce is vital to converting online visitors into paying customers. With GPT, you can efficiently generate engaging, informative, and SEO-friendly descriptions that showcase products and encourage purchases. This chapter will cover practical tips, examples, and resources for creating effective product descriptions, helping you maximise your earning potential in the e-commerce space.

How GPT Can Assist in Writing Product Descriptions

GPT is an invaluable tool for generating:

- **Engaging product descriptions** : Craft compelling descriptions that highlight a product's key features, benefits, and unique selling points (USPs).
- **SEO-optimised copy** : Create descriptions that include relevant keywords to improve product visibility in search engine results.
- **Consistent tone** : Maintain a consistent tone and style across a large catalogue of products, which is especially useful for e-commerce websites with hundreds or thousands of items.
- **Tailored descriptions for different audiences** : Adapt descriptions for different target markets or platforms, ensuring the language and style resonate with specific audiences.

Practical Tips to Maximise Earnings

1. **Highlight benefits, not just features** : Ensure GPT-generated product descriptions focus on how the product benefits the customer, not just listing technical specifications. For example, instead of "This jacket is waterproof," write, "Stay dry and

comfortable, whatever the weather, with our premium waterproof jacket."

2. **Incorporate SEO keywords** : Before generating content, conduct keyword research using tools like Google Keyword Planner or SEMrush. Provide these keywords to GPT to ensure that the descriptions are optimised for search engines, helping the product rank higher in search results.

3. **Focus on the target customer** : Tailor descriptions to the buyer's persona. For instance, a description for a high-end skincare product might use more luxurious language, while an eco-friendly product could emphasise sustainability and environmental impact.

4. **Keep it concise and clear** : Product descriptions should be short and easy to read. Use bullet points for technical details and keep sentences concise, ensuring that customers can quickly grasp the product's value.

5. **Create urgency with persuasive language** : Encourage customers to make a purchase by including phrases like "limited stock" or "only available for a short time," which can create a sense of urgency.

Example: Writing a Product Description for a Smartwatch

Suppose you need to create a product description for a new smartwatch. GPT can generate a description like this:

"Stay connected and active with the [Brand] Smartwatch. Track your heart rate, steps, and sleep quality while receiving real-time notifications from your phone. With its sleek design, water resistance, and long-lasting battery, it's perfect for both fitness enthusiasts and professionals on the go. Available now with free shipping. Don't miss out—order today!"

The description highlights the key benefits (tracking health metrics and staying connected), mentions essential features (design, water resistance, and battery life), and includes a call to action, all in a concise, customer-friendly format.

Resources to Boost Your Product Description Writing Business

- **SEO Tools** : Use tools like Ahrefs, Moz, or Google Keyword Planner to identify the most relevant keywords for the products you're describing.

- **E-commerce Platforms** : Familiarise yourself with popular platforms like Shopify, WooCommerce, and BigCommerce, as they often have specific formatting requirements for product descriptions.
- **GPT Integration** : OpenAI's GPT-4 API can streamline the process of generating product descriptions, allowing you to handle large catalogues efficiently.
- **Product Photography and Specifications** : Work closely with clients to obtain high-quality product images and detailed specifications, which will enhance the accuracy and appeal of the descriptions.

Maximising Earnings with E-commerce Product Descriptions

1. **Offer bulk services** : Many e-commerce businesses require descriptions for hundreds or thousands of products. Offer discounted rates for bulk orders, ensuring clients get value while you maximise your earnings through volume.
2. **Provide SEO-optimised packages** : Bundle your services with keyword research and SEO optimisation, charging higher rates

for descriptions that help improve product visibility on search engines.

3. **Specialise in niche markets** : Consider specialising in industries such as fashion, technology, beauty, or eco-friendly products. Niche expertise allows you to offer tailored descriptions, making your service more valuable to specific markets.

4. **Expand to other content types** : Offer additional services such as writing category descriptions, landing pages, and blog posts for e-commerce websites, increasing the scope of your work and income.

By using GPT for writing product descriptions, you can efficiently create high-quality, persuasive, and SEO-optimised content for a wide range of e-commerce products. Combining GPT's speed with your understanding of customer needs and SEO best practices will help you provide value to clients and significantly enhance your earning potential.

Chapter 8
Creating Online Course Content

The demand for online learning continues to grow, offering educators and content creators lucrative opportunities to develop courses on various subjects. GPT can help you efficiently generate high-quality, engaging, and structured online course content, from lesson plans to assessments, making the process faster and more scalable. This chapter provides practical tips, examples, and resources to help you maximise your earning potential by creating and selling online courses.

How GPT Can Assist in Creating Online Course Content

GPT can streamline many aspects of course creation, such as:

- **Lesson plans** : Generate detailed and organised lesson outlines for individual modules or entire courses.
- **Lecture scripts** : Write comprehensive scripts for video or audio lectures, ensuring clarity and engagement.
- **Quizzes and assessments** : Create questions and answers for quizzes, exams, or assessments, catering to various difficulty levels.
- **Course descriptions** : Write compelling and informative course descriptions that appeal to prospective students.

- **Study guides and resources** : Generate supplementary materials like study guides, worksheets, and reading lists to support learners.

Practical Tips to Maximise Earnings

1. **Focus on in-demand topics** : Research topics with high demand and low competition. Use tools like Udemy's Marketplace Insights or Google Trends to identify popular subjects in industries like technology, business, personal development, and health.
2. **Structure your content effectively** : Create well-structured courses with clear learning objectives. GPT can help generate outlines, but ensure that each module builds on the last, providing a logical learning progression.
3. **Use engaging language** : Make the content engaging and accessible. For example, instead of a dry, technical explanation, ask GPT to write in a conversational tone that simplifies complex concepts.
4. **Incorporate multimedia** : Create scripts for video and audio lectures, as well as written materials, to cater to different learning

styles. GPT can assist in generating content for these formats, but multimedia elements like visuals and animations will help keep learners engaged.

5. **Develop assessments** : Include quizzes, assignments, or practical projects to reinforce learning. GPT can create a range of multiple-choice questions, short answers, and case studies, but ensure these assessments are challenging enough to test students' understanding.

Example: Developing a Module for a Digital Marketing Course

Let's say you're creating an online course on digital marketing. GPT can help generate a module outline, such as:

- **Module Title** : "Introduction to SEO"

  - **Lesson 1** : What is SEO and Why It Matters
  - **Lesson 2** : Keyword Research and Selection
  - **Lesson 3** : On-Page SEO Best Practices

- **Lesson 4** : Building Backlinks and Authority
- **Lesson 5** : Measuring SEO Success

For each lesson, GPT can provide scripts or detailed explanations. For example, in Lesson 2, it might generate content like: "Keyword research is the foundation of any successful SEO strategy. It involves identifying the words and phrases your target audience is searching for. We'll explore tools like Google Keyword Planner and SEMrush to find the best keywords for your website."
The module can then be accompanied by quizzes, asking questions like, "Which tool is best for finding long-tail keywords?" with multiple-choice answers.

Resources to Boost Your Course Creation Business

- **Course Platforms** : Use platforms like Udemy, Teachable, and Coursera to host and sell your courses. These platforms often have tools that make it easy to upload content and track student progress.
- **Research Tools** : Use Udemy's Marketplace Insights, Google Trends, or Quora to research popular topics and

identify gaps in the market where you can create a unique course offering.

- **Multimedia Creation Tools** : Tools like Canva, Powtoon, and Camtasia can help you create visually appealing presentations and video content to supplement your written materials.
- **Quiz Creation Tools** : Platforms like Quizlet or Google Forms make it easy to create and manage quizzes, ensuring students engage with and retain the material.

Maximising Earnings with Online Course Content Creation

1. **Create a course bundle** : Offer a series of related courses as a bundle, covering beginner to advanced levels. This can attract students who want to follow a comprehensive learning path and increase your overall sales.
2. **Sell on multiple platforms** : Upload your course on various platforms, such as Udemy, Skillshare, or your own website, to reach a wider audience and maximise your earnings.
3. **Offer certificates** : Students are often willing to pay more for courses that provide

a certificate of completion, which they can add to their CV or LinkedIn profile. Offer certification to make your course more appealing.

4. **Monetise add-ons** : Include extra resources like one-on-one coaching, downloadable workbooks, or live Q&A sessions, which you can charge extra for. These services add value to your course and give you another revenue stream.

5. **Focus on niche topics** : If you have expertise in a niche subject, consider creating courses that serve a specialised audience. Niche courses tend to have less competition, allowing you to charge a premium price.

By leveraging GPT to efficiently generate structured, informative, and engaging course content, you can produce high-quality online courses that attract a wide audience. Combined with the right marketing strategies and add-on services, you can significantly boost your earning potential in the growing online education market.

Chapter 9
Developing Tutorials and Guides

Creating high-quality tutorials and guides is an effective way to help others master new skills or understand complex topics. With the help of GPT, you can quickly generate clear, informative, and engaging tutorials or step-by-step guides for various subjects. This chapter offers practical tips, examples, and resources to help you maximise your earning potential through the development of tutorials and guides.

How GPT Can Assist in Developing Tutorials and Guides

GPT can help streamline the process of creating tutorials by:

- **Generating step-by-step instructions** : Provide detailed, easy-to-follow instructions for processes, making the content accessible for learners at different skill levels.
- **Clarifying complex concepts** : Simplify complex topics by generating concise explanations, breaking down information into manageable pieces.
- **Creating content for various formats** : GPT can assist with the generation of

written, video, or visual tutorials, adapting content to suit different learning preferences.

- **Tailoring to different audiences** : GPT can help customise tutorials for beginners, intermediate learners, or advanced users, ensuring that your guides are appropriate for the target audience.

Practical Tips to Maximise Earnings

1. **Identify popular topics** : Focus on creating tutorials for in-demand topics. Research common problems or questions people have in your chosen niche using tools like Google Trends, Quora, or Reddit. GPT can then generate content around these specific issues, ensuring the tutorial addresses a relevant need.
2. **Create clear and concise content** : Use GPT to generate simple, clear instructions that are easy to follow. Avoid jargon, unless your audience is advanced, and focus on a logical, step-by-step approach to help users solve their problems effectively.
3. **Use visuals to enhance tutorials** : When writing instructions or guides, incorporate visuals, such as screenshots, diagrams, or

videos, to make the process easier to follow. You can create the visual components manually, but GPT can assist with generating captions or explanations.

4. **Update content regularly** : Ensure that your tutorials remain relevant by updating them frequently, especially for tech-related topics. GPT can quickly generate updated sections or new content when processes change.

5. **Optimise for search engines** : Use SEO techniques to make your tutorials more discoverable. Conduct keyword research and use GPT to seamlessly incorporate these terms into the tutorial, improving the chances of your content ranking high in search results.

Example: Writing a Guide on Using a Design Tool

Let's say you're creating a tutorial for a design tool like Canva. GPT can help generate an easy-to-follow guide, such as:

Title : "How to Create a Professional Social Media Graphic in Canva"

Step 1 : Open Canva and choose a template Explanation: "Log in to Canva, and under the 'Social Media' section, select a template that fits your brand's style. You can also search for templates using keywords like 'Instagram' or 'Facebook cover.'"

Step 2 : Customise the design

Explanation: "Click on any element of the template, such as text, images, or shapes, to customise them. Upload your own images or use Canva's free library to replace placeholders."

Step 3 : Adjust colours and fonts

Explanation: "Select your brand's colours and fonts by clicking the colour and font options in the toolbar. Use Canva's brand kit feature to store your colours and fonts for future use."

This step-by-step guide is simple, easy to follow, and includes actionable tips.

Resources to Boost Your Tutorial and Guide Development

- **Content Research Tools** : Tools like AnswerThePublic and Ubersuggest can help identify popular questions and topics that users are searching for, giving you ideas for tutorials.
- **Tutorial Platforms** : Consider publishing your guides on platforms like Medium, YouTube, or your own blog. These platforms are great for reaching a large audience, and

they can be monetised through ads or sponsored content.

- **Video Tutorial Software** : Tools like Loom, OBS Studio, or Camtasia can be used to create video versions of your tutorials, adding more value to your content.
- **Visual Design Tools** : Use Canva or Snagit to create supporting visuals such as infographics, flowcharts, or step-by-step diagrams to complement your written tutorials.

Maximising Earnings with Tutorial and Guide Development

1. **Monetise through platforms** : Upload your tutorials to monetised platforms such as YouTube, where you can earn through ads or sponsored content. Alternatively, publish written guides on blogs with affiliate links or sponsored posts.
2. **Sell premium tutorials** : Package your best tutorials or create in-depth, step-by-step guides as e-books or video courses. Sell these as premium content on platforms like Gumroad, Teachable, or Udemy, where users are willing to pay for high-quality, structured learning.

3. **Offer custom tutorials** : Offer personalised tutorials for clients in niche industries who need tailored guidance. Charge a premium for creating bespoke guides or providing one-on-one tutorials.
4. **Create multi-format content** : Diversify your offerings by creating tutorials in different formats (e.g., written, video, interactive), catering to various learning styles. This allows you to sell across multiple platforms and increase your income streams.
5. **Affiliate marketing** : If you're creating guides for software, tools, or online platforms, join affiliate programs to promote these products in your tutorials. You can earn commissions when readers or viewers make purchases through your links.

By using GPT to develop tutorials and guides, you can create high-quality, detailed content that addresses the needs of your target audience. With the right marketing and monetisation strategies, you can turn your tutorials into a consistent source of income, capitalising on the growing demand for educational content across various industries.

Chapter 10

Ghostwriting Services

Ghostwriting is the practice of writing content on behalf of someone else, where the client gets credit for the work. Offering ghostwriting services can be a highly lucrative career, as it allows you to work on a variety of projects—such as books, blog posts, speeches, and articles—without the need for personal recognition. This chapter provides practical tips, examples, and resources to help you maximise your earning potential as a ghostwriter.

How GPT Can Assist in Ghostwriting

GPT can significantly streamline the ghostwriting process, offering:

- **Fast content generation** : Help create drafts or full pieces for a wide range of formats, including articles, reports, books, and more.
- **Consistent tone and style** : Tailor writing to match the voice of the client or brand, ensuring the final product is indistinguishable from their personal style.

- **Research assistance** : Provide relevant facts, examples, or background information for writing projects.
- **Editing and revisions** : Offer suggestions for improving clarity, flow, and engagement in written content.

Practical Tips to Maximise Earnings

1. **Diversify your services** : Ghostwriting encompasses a wide variety of content types, including books, blog posts, speeches, articles, and newsletters. By offering multiple types of services, you can attract clients with different needs, broadening your earning potential.
2. **Specialise in high-demand niches** : Focus on writing for niche markets with strong demand. For example, ghostwriting for business executives, politicians, or influencers often pays higher rates than general content writing. Find a niche that aligns with your strengths, such as self-help books, business reports, or autobiographies.
3. **Match the client's tone and voice** : One of the key skills in ghostwriting is writing in a way that sounds authentic to the client. GPT

can help you adapt your style to match your client's, but be sure to study their existing content closely to understand their unique voice.

4. **Set clear expectations** : Define the scope of the project, including deadlines, revisions, and fees, at the outset. Use contracts to ensure both parties understand the terms and that you are fairly compensated for your time and effort.

5. **Maintain confidentiality** : As a ghostwriter, protecting your client's anonymity is critical. Ensure that all agreements include non-disclosure clauses, which can also justify charging higher rates for more confidential projects.

Example: Ghostwriting a Self-Help Book

Imagine a client hires you to ghostwrite a self-help book. GPT can help generate chapter outlines, create drafts, and even suggest motivational language. For instance, the chapter "Overcoming Procrastination" could include a practical, step-by-step guide on breaking down tasks, improving focus, and building momentum. You could provide the client with a full manuscript and offer revisions to ensure the content aligns with their vision.

A sample outline for the book might look like this:

- **Chapter 1** : Identifying Procrastination Habits
- **Chapter 2** : Why We Procrastinate
- **Chapter 3** : Techniques for Breaking the Habit
- **Chapter 4** : Staying Productive and Focused

Each chapter could include personal anecdotes, case studies, and action steps to engage readers and provide valuable, actionable content.

Resources to Boost Your Ghostwriting Business

- **Freelancing Platforms** : Websites like Upwork, Freelancer, and Reedsy are great places to find ghostwriting clients, especially for projects like e-books, memoirs, and business writing.
- **Contracts and Non-Disclosure Agreements** : Ensure you use contracts to protect your rights and income. Sites like LegalZoom or Rocket Lawyer offer

templates for freelance contracts, including non-disclosure agreements.

- **Writing Tools** : Use tools like Grammarly for grammar and style checks, and Scrivener or Google Docs for organising long-form content like books or reports.
- **Professional Associations** : Join ghostwriting organisations like the Association of Ghostwriters, which can provide networking opportunities, job leads, and professional development resources.

Maximising Earnings with Ghostwriting Services

1. **Charge premium rates for books and long-form content** : Ghostwriting a book or long-form content requires significant effort and time. Charge premium rates for these projects, and if possible, negotiate royalties or co-writing credit on books, which can provide long-term income.
2. **Offer value-added services** : Provide additional services such as editing, proofreading, or even publishing consultation to clients. Offering a full package can increase your earnings and provide clients with more value.

3. **Build long-term relationships** : Aim for repeat clients, particularly those in need of ongoing content, such as bloggers, business executives, or public figures. Offering retainer agreements ensures you have a steady income and long-term projects.

4. **Target corporate clients** : Ghostwriting for executives or corporations can be extremely profitable. Many businesses need white papers, reports, and speeches written on their behalf, and they are often willing to pay more for high-quality work.

5. **Leverage testimonials and referrals** : Once you've completed a few projects, ask satisfied clients for testimonials or referrals. Many high-paying clients come through word-of-mouth, especially in specialised industries.

By offering ghostwriting services, you can work on diverse projects while allowing clients to take the credit. Using GPT to enhance productivity and creativity, combined with strategic pricing and marketing, will help you build a successful and lucrative ghostwriting business.

Chapter 11
Writing Newsletters

Newsletters remain a powerful tool for businesses, influencers, and individuals to engage their audiences. Writing effective newsletters requires a clear understanding of the audience, compelling content, and consistency. Using GPT, you can streamline the creation process, helping clients maintain regular communication while boosting your earning potential. This chapter provides practical tips, examples, and resources to help you succeed in writing newsletters.

How GPT Can Assist in Newsletter Writing

GPT can significantly simplify and enhance newsletter writing by:

- **Generating content ideas** : Offer creative suggestions for newsletter topics based on industry trends or client needs.
- **Tailoring content to specific audiences** : Adapt the tone, style, and content to match the target audience, ensuring engagement and relevance.
- **Creating engaging subject lines** : Craft compelling subject lines that increase open rates.

- **Writing and formatting content** : Help generate polished, structured content that is easy to read and visually appealing.
- **Suggesting calls to action (CTAs)** : Propose effective CTAs that encourage readers to take specific actions, such as signing up, purchasing a product, or visiting a website.

Practical Tips to Maximise Earnings

1. **Identify and cater to niche markets** : Specialising in a particular industry (e.g., tech, health, finance) allows you to understand the unique needs of the audience. Newsletters in specialised fields often command higher rates due to the expertise required.
2. **Create consistent content** : A successful newsletter needs to be delivered on a regular schedule, whether weekly, bi-weekly, or monthly. Offer retainer packages to clients, ensuring consistent income by managing their entire newsletter strategy.
3. **Focus on audience engagement** : Write content that resonates with the readers. Encourage interaction by asking for

feedback, including polls or surveys, and ensuring the content is both valuable and relevant.

4. **Optimise subject lines and previews** : The subject line is crucial for enticing readers to open the email. Experiment with different styles, including questions, teasers, or personalised greetings. GPT can help generate variations to test for effectiveness.

5. **Incorporate storytelling** : Use stories to make newsletters more relatable and engaging. Whether it's a personal anecdote or a customer success story, storytelling can captivate readers and keep them subscribed.

6. **Track performance and adjust** : Analyse open rates, click-through rates, and engagement metrics to improve future newsletters. GPT can help you rephrase and rewrite content to better align with what the audience prefers.

Example: Writing a Monthly Marketing Newsletter

Let's say you're writing a monthly newsletter for a digital marketing agency. GPT can help generate topics like:

- **Subject Line** : "5 Marketing Trends You Can't Afford to Miss This Month"

Newsletter Content Outline :

- **Introduction** : A brief welcome note discussing the current marketing landscape, trends, or recent industry news.
- **Main Article** : "5 Key Marketing Trends for 2024"—A summary of emerging trends, such as the rise of AI in marketing, the importance of video content, and data privacy issues.
- **Client Success Story** : Highlight a recent success, such as how a business increased its conversion rates using a specific marketing strategy.
- **Call to Action** : Encourage readers to book a free consultation or download a white paper on improving their digital marketing efforts.

GPT can help structure the entire newsletter, generating copy that is informative, engaging, and encourages readers to take action.

Resources to Boost Your Newsletter Writing Business

- **Email Marketing Platforms** : Tools like Mailchimp, ConvertKit, and Constant Contact help automate newsletter distribution, track performance metrics, and segment audiences for better targeting.
- **Headline Generators** : Tools like CoSchedule's Headline Analyzer or GPT itself can help create effective subject lines and headlines.
- **Analytics Tools** : Use Google Analytics or the reporting tools in your email platform to track newsletter performance, helping you refine your strategy for clients.
- **Freelancing Platforms** : Websites like Fiverr, Upwork, or LinkedIn allow you to advertise your newsletter writing services and connect with potential clients.

Maximising Earnings with Newsletter Writing

1. **Offer tiered pricing** : Provide different packages depending on the length, frequency, and complexity of the newsletter. For example, charge more for a weekly

newsletter with multiple sections than a simpler monthly update.

2. **Create a portfolio** : Showcase your best work in a portfolio to attract new clients. Include examples of successful newsletters with metrics such as high open rates or conversion statistics to demonstrate your value.

3. **Upsell content strategy services** : Alongside writing, offer newsletter strategy services, including content planning, audience segmentation, and performance analysis. This adds value for clients and allows you to charge higher fees.

4. **Target small businesses and influencers** : Small businesses and individual influencers often need consistent newsletters but may not have the time or expertise to write them. Offering tailored packages to these clients can provide a reliable income stream.

5. **Create automated email sequences** : Beyond one-off newsletters, offer to create automated email campaigns, such as welcome sequences or drip campaigns. These can help businesses nurture leads or engage customers over time, allowing you to charge more for the extended service.

6. **Affiliate marketing** : If applicable, include affiliate links in newsletters where you can

earn commissions for products or services recommended to readers.

By using GPT to streamline content creation and tailoring your services to the needs of clients, you can provide high-quality newsletters that engage audiences. Offering additional services, retaining clients on long-term contracts, and optimising content based on performance will enable you to maximise your earning potential as a newsletter writer.

Chapter 12
AI-Powered Script Writing for Videos

Video content is an increasingly popular medium for storytelling, marketing, education, and entertainment. Writing effective scripts requires creativity, structure, and engagement. With AI-powered tools like GPT, the scriptwriting process can be made more efficient and scalable, allowing writers to produce high-quality scripts quickly. This chapter offers practical tips, examples, and resources to help you maximise your earning potential as an AI-powered scriptwriter for videos.

How GPT Can Assist in Script Writing

GPT can be a powerful tool for generating scripts by:

- **Outlining and structuring scripts** : Quickly create detailed outlines that form the backbone of the video script.
- **Generating dialogue** : Write natural-sounding conversations, enhancing character interactions in scripted videos.
- **Adapting tone and style** : Tailor the tone of the script to suit the video format, whether it's educational, promotional, or entertainment-based.
- **Providing visual prompts** : Suggest ideas for visual elements, enhancing the storytelling aspect of the video.
- **Brainstorming ideas** : Provide inspiration for plotlines, story arcs, or dialogue based on a topic or theme, helping writers overcome creative blocks.

Practical Tips to Maximise Earnings

1. **Target niche industries** : Specialise in writing scripts for specific niches, such as explainer videos, e-learning content, corporate training, or YouTube channels. Niches like corporate training or promotional content for businesses can command higher fees.
2. **Offer full-service packages** : Provide scriptwriting along with storyboarding or video production consulting. Clients often prefer end-to-end solutions, and by bundling services, you can charge more.
3. **Collaborate with video creators** : Partner with YouTubers, marketing agencies, or production companies. Consistent collaboration can lead to long-term projects, ensuring a stable income.
4. **Focus on storytelling** : Video scripts are most effective when they engage the audience through storytelling. Use GPT to help create compelling narratives that draw viewers in, whether it's a brand story, testimonial, or educational video.
5. **Experiment with different formats** : Write scripts for various types of video content—product demos, how-to guides, social media ads, or web series. By diversifying your

expertise, you open up opportunities in different markets.

6. **Tailor scripts to the platform** : Ensure that the scripts you write are optimised for the platform they will appear on. For example, YouTube videos may require catchy openings to retain viewers, while Instagram reels might need short, snappy lines. GPT can help you adapt content to different formats quickly.

Example: Writing a Script for a YouTube Product Review Video

Let's assume a client wants a script for a product review video on YouTube. GPT can help create an engaging script that highlights key features of the product, engages the audience, and includes clear calls to action.

Outline :

- **Introduction (10-15 seconds)** : "Welcome back to [Channel Name]! Today, we're reviewing the all-new [Product Name], a game-changer in [industry]. Let's dive into its top features."
- **Product Overview (1-2 minutes)** : Describe the product, its uses, and why it stands out

in the market. GPT can generate engaging, informative content that highlights key benefits.

- **User Experience (1 minute)** : Add a personal touch by sharing a user story or case study of how the product performed.
- **Comparison (30 seconds)** : Briefly compare the product to others in the market, highlighting its advantages.
- **Call to Action (15-20 seconds)** : "If you found this review helpful, make sure to hit the like button and subscribe for more reviews! You can also check out [Product Name] using the link in the description below."

This format ensures that the script is structured to keep the audience engaged while providing useful information in a digestible manner.

Resources to Boost Your Scriptwriting Business

- **Video Platforms** : YouTube, Vimeo, and TikTok are great platforms to explore video trends and identify the type of content that gets traction. Writing scripts tailored to these platforms will help you understand what resonates with audiences.

- **AI Writing Tools** : Use GPT-powered tools like Jasper or Copy.ai, alongside GPT, to help generate content ideas and scripts for videos.
- **Script Formatting Software** : Tools like Final Draft, Celtx, or Google Docs can help organise scripts into professional formats that are easy to share with clients.
- **Freelance Platforms** : Websites like Fiverr, Upwork, or Scripted can help you find clients looking for scriptwriting services, allowing you to advertise your expertise in AI-powered content generation.

Maximising Earnings with Script Writing

1. **Charge by script length or complexity** : Offer pricing based on the length and complexity of the script. Shorter scripts for promotional videos may be charged at a lower rate, while longer or more intricate scripts for documentaries or video series should be priced higher.
2. **Create templates for common formats** : Develop reusable templates for common video formats like product reviews, explainer videos, or social media ads. These

templates will allow you to quickly customise scripts for clients, saving time and increasing productivity.

3. **Provide multilingual scripts** : Offer services to create scripts in multiple languages using GPT's language translation abilities. This expands your market and allows you to charge more for bilingual or multilingual projects.

4. **Offer revision services** : Include a set number of revisions in your pricing or offer additional revisions for a fee. Clients often need scripts tailored to specific brand messaging, and offering revisions ensures client satisfaction while boosting your earnings.

5. **Build a portfolio of successful scripts** : Compile examples of scripts that have been produced into successful videos. Include metrics like view counts, engagement rates, or conversion statistics to demonstrate the impact of your work to potential clients.

6. **Leverage video SEO** : Ensure your scripts are optimised for search engines by including relevant keywords that will help the video rank higher on platforms like YouTube. GPT can assist in generating keyword-rich content to improve video discoverability, adding value to your service.

Additional Revenue Streams

1. **Create educational content** : Offer online courses or workshops teaching AI-powered scriptwriting for aspiring video creators. Platforms like Udemy or Skillshare can be used to monetise these courses.
2. **Affiliate marketing** : For YouTube or social media video scripts, include affiliate links in the script that direct viewers to products or services. You can earn commissions through these referrals if the client allows for affiliate promotions in their videos.
3. **Sell pre-made scripts** : Write generic scripts for popular niches such as beauty tutorials, tech reviews, or fitness content, and sell them on marketplaces like Etsy or Fiverr. Clients looking for quick, ready-to-use scripts will appreciate these offerings.

By using GPT to streamline the scriptwriting process, you can produce high-quality content efficiently, opening up new opportunities in video production. With the right pricing, marketing, and diversification strategies, you can maximise your earning potential in AI-powered script writing for videos.

Chapter 13

Website Content Generation

Website content is the backbone of a company's online presence, helping to inform, engage, and convert visitors. Creating high-quality content for websites involves writing pages such as homepages, service descriptions, blogs, FAQs, and more. With the help of AI tools like GPT, you can streamline the content generation process, making it easier to produce polished, SEO-friendly content at scale. This summary outlines practical tips, examples, and resources to help you maximise your earning potential in website content creation.

How GPT Can Assist in Website Content Generation

GPT offers a range of features that can enhance the content creation process for websites, such as:

- **Generating SEO-optimised content** : GPT can help you create keyword-rich copy that improves search engine rankings.
- **Writing tailored content** : It can adapt content to suit different industries, audiences, and tones, ensuring relevancy and engagement.

- **Outlining pages** : Quickly generate outlines for essential web pages like homepages, service descriptions, or product listings, structuring information for clarity and flow.
- **Creating call-to-action (CTA) prompts** : Provide engaging CTAs that encourage users to take action, whether it's signing up, purchasing, or contacting the business.
- **Rewriting existing content** : GPT can revise or rephrase existing website copy to improve readability, update outdated information, or optimise it for SEO.

Practical Tips to Maximise Earnings

1. **Offer full-site content packages** : Rather than just creating one-off pages, offer packages that include all core website pages (home, about, services, contact) and even blog posts or FAQs. These packages command higher fees and provide clients with a comprehensive service.
2. **Tailor content for different niches** : Specialise in writing content for specific industries, such as healthcare, e-commerce, or finance. Each industry has unique

requirements, and expertise in a niche will allow you to charge premium rates.

3. **Focus on SEO** : Website content needs to be optimised for search engines. GPT can help you create content that includes target keywords, meta descriptions, and headers. By offering SEO-optimised content, you increase the value of your services.

4. **Incorporate user experience (UX) principles** : Ensure that content is easy to navigate and understand, catering to the user journey. Well-structured content that guides users through a website smoothly can improve engagement and conversion rates.

5. **Regular updates and content refresh** : Offer content refresh services to keep websites updated with current trends, statistics, or SEO improvements. Ongoing work with clients can provide a steady stream of income.

Example: Writing Content for an E-commerce Website

For an e-commerce website, GPT can assist in generating product descriptions, category pages, and landing pages.

Homepage Example :

- **Headline** : "Discover Premium Quality [Product Category] – Affordable and Delivered Fast."
- **Intro** : Introduce the brand, the quality of the products, and the range of items available.
- **Product Highlights** : Briefly outline the top products with short descriptions, showcasing the most popular items.
- **CTA** : "Browse our collection now and get free shipping on all orders over £50."

Product Page Example :

- **Product Name** : [Product Name]
- **Description** : Write a compelling description highlighting the features, benefits, and unique selling points of the product.
- **Specifications** : Detail size, material, or technical specifications.
- **CTA** : "Add to Cart – Free Returns Within 30 Days."

GPT can help with writing engaging and informative product descriptions that drive conversions, ensuring the website effectively showcases products and services.

Resources to Boost Your Website Content Generation Business

- **SEO Tools** : Use tools like SEMrush, Ahrefs, or Ubersuggest to identify high-ranking keywords and optimise website content for search engines.
- **Website Builders** : Familiarise yourself with platforms like WordPress, Wix, or Shopify. Offering content tailored to these platforms adds value, as many clients need website content integrated seamlessly into their site's design.
- **Freelancing Platforms** : Platforms like Fiverr, Upwork, and PeoplePerHour can help you connect with businesses in need of website content creation services.
- **Content Management Systems (CMS)** : Learn how to work with CMS platforms like WordPress and HubSpot to directly upload content for clients, providing added convenience and allowing you to charge more for integrated services.

Maximising Earnings with Website Content Generation

1. **Charge by word count or project scope** : Offer flexible pricing models based on word count, page length, or the total number of pages required. Complex content, such as service pages or product descriptions, may warrant higher fees due to the research and SEO considerations involved.
2. **Offer ongoing content creation services** : Websites need fresh content to remain competitive. Provide ongoing services such as blog writing, updating landing pages, or refreshing product descriptions. This can create a steady stream of income through monthly retainers.
3. **Provide additional services** : Offer related services like content auditing, proofreading, or UX copywriting to increase your value to clients. Bundling services together allows you to charge more for comprehensive packages.
4. **Target local businesses** : Many small and medium businesses need professional website content to compete online but may not have in-house writers. Offer competitive packages to local companies, showcasing

the benefits of professionally written, SEO-optimised content.

5. **Create industry-specific templates** : Develop website content templates for particular industries (e.g., healthcare, real estate, SaaS). These templates can help you quickly produce high-quality content while maintaining consistency, allowing you to serve more clients efficiently.

Additional Revenue Streams

1. **Blog writing for SEO** : Offer blog writing services as part of the content generation strategy. Regular blog posts can boost search engine rankings, improve brand authority, and increase traffic, allowing you to charge more for this ongoing service.

2. **Landing page optimisation** : In addition to general website content, create and optimise landing pages designed for specific campaigns, increasing the chances of user conversion.

3. **Content updates** : Offer a retainer service to update or refresh website content regularly to ensure it stays current and relevant.

4. **Content strategy consulting** : Offer consulting services where you help clients develop a long-term content strategy to support their business goals, including a plan for SEO, blogging, and social media integration.

By leveraging GPT for website content generation, you can produce high-quality, SEO-optimised copy efficiently, allowing you to take on more clients and scale your business. Offering a range of services, from complete site content to ongoing blog writing, ensures that you can maximise your earning potential while providing value to your clients.

Chapter 14
Writing E-books for Passive Income

E-books provide a fantastic opportunity to generate passive income, especially in the digital age. By creating high-quality e-books on subjects that interest you or serve a specific market need, you can create an ongoing revenue stream. With the help of AI tools like GPT, the process of writing e-books can be streamlined, allowing you to produce content faster while maintaining quality. This summary outlines practical tips, examples, and resources to help you maximise your earning potential through e-book writing.

How GPT Can Assist in Writing E-books

GPT offers several advantages in the e-book writing process:

- **Generating ideas and outlines** : GPT can help you brainstorm e-book ideas based on popular trends or your areas of expertise. It can also create detailed chapter outlines, giving structure to the content.
- **Content creation** : From writing complete chapters to filling in specific sections, GPT can help generate clear, engaging text for your e-book.
- **Editing and rewriting** : AI can assist in refining your content, suggesting improvements, and ensuring consistency in tone, style, and flow.
- **Research assistance** : GPT can summarise complex topics or provide additional information to ensure your e-book is well-researched and credible.
- **Formatting and layout suggestions** : While not a design tool, GPT can provide

recommendations for organising your content in a way that is logical and easy to follow for readers.

Practical Tips to Maximise Earnings from E-books

1. **Choose a profitable niche** : Research popular topics or niches that have high demand but low competition. Subjects like self-improvement, entrepreneurship, health, and finance tend to sell well. Use platforms like Amazon Kindle or Udemy to identify trends.
2. **Write for a specific audience** : Tailor your content to a specific group, such as beginners in a particular field or professionals looking for advanced knowledge. Writing for a niche market can help your e-book stand out and appeal to a targeted audience.
3. **Create high-quality content** : Even if you are using AI to help with the writing process, ensure that the content is valuable, informative, and well-organised. Poorly written e-books can result in negative reviews, which will harm your sales.
4. **Utilise SEO and keywords** : Incorporate relevant keywords in your e-book title,

description, and content to make it more discoverable on platforms like Amazon. GPT can help you generate keyword-rich copy, ensuring that your e-book is optimised for search engines.

5. **Design an appealing cover** : Although the content is essential, the cover design can significantly impact your e-book's success. Consider hiring a graphic designer or using design tools like Canva to create a professional and eye-catching cover.

6. **Price strategically** : Start with a lower price to gain reviews and traction, then gradually increase the price once the e-book has gained some popularity. Alternatively, offer discounts during promotional periods to boost visibility.

Example: Writing an E-book on Personal Finance

Let's say you decide to write an e-book on personal finance for beginners. GPT can help you:

- **Outline the book** : "Budgeting Basics for Beginners" could include chapters on creating a budget, saving for emergencies, managing debt, and investing for the future.

- **Generate content** : Each chapter could begin with an introduction generated by GPT, followed by step-by-step advice and practical tips. For example, a section on debt management might explain different types of debt, strategies for paying off loans, and the benefits of consolidating debt.
- **CTA at the end of each chapter** : Encourage readers to take specific actions, such as downloading a budget template or signing up for your email list for more financial tips.

Resources to Boost Your E-book Writing Business

- **Amazon Kindle Direct Publishing (KDP)** : One of the best platforms for self-publishing e-books, allowing you to reach a global audience. KDP offers easy-to-use tools for formatting, publishing, and marketing your e-books.
- **Draft2Digital** : A publishing platform that distributes e-books across multiple retailers, including Amazon, Barnes & Noble, and Apple Books.

- **Design Tools** : Use Canva or Adobe Spark for creating professional e-book covers and promotional graphics.
- **Keyword Research Tools** : Tools like Publisher Rocket or Ubersuggest can help identify profitable keywords for your e-book title and description, improving visibility on search platforms.
- **Freelance Platforms** : Websites like Fiverr or Upwork allow you to outsource parts of the e-book production process, such as cover design, editing, or marketing, saving time and ensuring quality.

Maximising Earnings from E-books

1. **Publish multiple e-books** : The more e-books you publish, the more income streams you generate. Consider writing a series of e-books on related topics to build a collection that appeals to readers interested in a particular niche.
2. **Create companion products** : Bundle your e-book with related resources such as workbooks, templates, or checklists. Offering additional content can increase the

perceived value and allow you to charge a higher price.

3. **Leverage email marketing** : Build an email list of readers and potential buyers. Offer them exclusive discounts, sneak peeks, or early access to your next e-book to encourage repeat purchases.

4. **Run promotions and discounts** : Periodically offer your e-book at a discounted rate to boost sales and visibility, especially during peak shopping periods like holidays or special events.

5. **Monetise through affiliate marketing** : Include affiliate links in your e-book for products or services relevant to the content. If readers purchase through these links, you can earn a commission, adding another layer of passive income.

6. **Repurpose content** : Break down sections of your e-book into blog posts, social media content, or YouTube videos to promote the e-book and drive traffic to the purchase page.

Additional Revenue Streams

1. **Offer consulting or coaching** : Position yourself as an expert by offering consulting

or coaching services related to the topic of your e-book. Readers may be willing to pay for one-on-one guidance, further increasing your income.

2. **Create an audiobook version** : Convert your e-book into an audiobook using platforms like Audible, giving you access to another audience and boosting your passive income potential.

3. **Develop an online course** : Turn the content of your e-book into an online course on platforms like Udemy or Teachable. By repurposing the material, you can charge a higher price for a more interactive learning experience.

4. **Licensing** : Consider offering your e-book to businesses or educational institutions for licensing. They may purchase bulk copies or distribute it as part of a course or training programme, providing you with consistent revenue.

By leveraging GPT and following a strategic approach to writing, marketing, and selling e-books, you can create a lucrative passive income stream. Diversifying your content, expanding your audience, and offering related services or products will help you maximise your earning potential as an e-book author.

Chapter 15
Proofreading and Editing Services

Offering proofreading and editing services is a valuable way to earn a consistent income by helping individuals and businesses polish their written content. With the rise of digital content and self-publishing, the demand for high-quality proofreading and editing services has increased significantly. This summary outlines how you can offer these services effectively, includes practical tips for enhancing your offerings, and provides examples and resources to help you maximise your earning potential.

How GPT Can Assist in Proofreading and Editing

While AI tools like GPT cannot entirely replace human expertise in proofreading and editing, they can assist in several key areas:

- **Basic grammar and spelling checks** : GPT can identify and suggest corrections for grammatical errors, misspellings, and punctuation mistakes.

- **Sentence restructuring** : It can suggest alternative sentence structures to improve clarity and flow.
- **Style adjustments** : GPT can help maintain consistency in tone and writing style, especially when working with large documents.
- **Content enhancement** : The tool can offer suggestions for enriching the text, making it more engaging or informative.
- **Efficiency** : GPT can quickly scan through large volumes of text to highlight potential issues, allowing you to focus on more nuanced editing work.

Practical Tips to Maximise Earnings from Proofreading and Editing

1. **Specialise in a niche** : Specialising in a particular area, such as academic papers, business documents, fiction, or website content, can help you stand out in a crowded market. Niche expertise allows you to charge premium rates as clients value your specific knowledge.

2. **Set clear service levels** : Offer different service packages to accommodate various client needs. For example, you could offer:

   - **Basic proofreading** : A simple check for grammar, spelling, and punctuation.
   - **Editing** : More in-depth work that includes sentence restructuring, tone adjustment, and improving clarity.
   - **Substantive or developmental editing** : A thorough review of the document's structure, argument flow, and content quality. This is especially useful for long-form content like novels or academic theses.

3. **Offer fast turnaround times** : Many clients need quick proofreading and editing, especially for business and academic purposes. Offering expedited services (at a higher fee) can boost your earnings.

4. **Use editing tools** : While GPT can assist with basic tasks, use specialised tools like Grammarly, ProWritingAid, or Hemingway Editor to provide an additional layer of accuracy and professionalism in your proofreading and editing work.

5. **Maintain regular communication with clients** : Keep your clients updated on the

progress of their work, and offer suggestions or ask for clarifications to ensure the final product meets their expectations. Good communication increases client satisfaction and the likelihood of repeat business.

Example: Proofreading a Business Document

Suppose you are hired to proofread a company's marketing brochure. Here's how you can approach it:

- **Basic proofreading** : You begin by scanning for obvious errors in grammar, punctuation, and spelling.
- **Clarity and tone check** : You ensure that the language is clear, concise, and professional, aligned with the company's brand voice.
- **Consistency review** : You check for consistency in terminology, formatting, and use of capitalisation across the document.
- **Final suggestions** : Offer minor improvements in word choice and sentence flow to make the content more engaging and persuasive.

By offering detailed feedback and suggestions beyond basic proofreading, you provide added value to your client, justifying higher rates.

Resources to Boost Your Proofreading and Editing Services

- **Grammarly** : A popular tool that helps identify grammar, punctuation, and syntax errors. Use this alongside your manual editing to improve accuracy and efficiency.
- **ProWritingAid** : This tool provides more in-depth grammar and style suggestions and is excellent for longer documents like novels or research papers.
- **Chicago Manual of Style / APA Style Guide** : Ensure you are familiar with different style guides, especially if you are offering services to academic or corporate clients who follow specific citation or formatting standards.
- **Reedsy** : A platform for freelance editors and proofreaders, particularly those working with authors. It can help you connect with self-publishing writers in need of professional editing.

- **Freelancing Platforms** : Use platforms like Fiverr, Upwork, and PeoplePerHour to offer your services and gain visibility among clients looking for quick, reliable proofreading and editing help.

Maximising Earnings in Proofreading and Editing

1. **Charge per word or per project** : While some editors charge by the hour, charging per word or per project can make pricing more transparent for clients and easier for you to calculate. Complex documents, such as academic papers or technical reports, can warrant higher rates.
2. **Offer subscription services** : For clients who regularly produce content (such as bloggers, businesses, or academics), offer a subscription service for ongoing proofreading and editing. This ensures steady work and income.
3. **Build long-term relationships** : Focus on developing long-term relationships with clients. Repeat business can be more profitable and easier to manage than constantly seeking new clients.

4. **Expand into related services** : In addition to proofreading and editing, offer services such as content writing, ghostwriting, or formatting for e-books or academic papers. This broadens your offering and allows you to cater to a wider range of client needs.
5. **Target self-published authors** : With the rise of self-publishing, many authors are looking for affordable, high-quality editing services. Specialising in manuscript editing for self-publishers can lead to consistent work and good pay.

Additional Revenue Streams

1. **Content creation for clients** : Some clients may require help rewriting sections of their documents. Offering a rewriting service alongside proofreading can increase your income, as it involves more detailed work.
2. **Academic editing services** : Academic papers often require strict adherence to style guides and may involve checking for citations and formatting. By specialising in academic editing, you can charge higher rates due to the precision and expertise required.

3. **Offering workshops or courses** : If you have advanced editing skills, consider offering workshops or online courses teaching others how to improve their proofreading and editing abilities. This can create another stream of passive income.
4. **Editing for digital platforms** : Many businesses need help editing website copy, blog posts, or newsletters. By offering editing services tailored to online content (with a focus on SEO and readability), you can appeal to a growing digital market.

By positioning yourself as a professional proofreader and editor, utilising AI tools like GPT to streamline your processes, and offering a range of services tailored to different client needs, you can establish a successful business. Combining your expertise with technology and effective marketing strategies will help you attract a wide array of clients and maximise your earning potential.

Chapter 16
Translating Text Using GPT

With the rise of AI technologies like GPT, translating text has become more efficient, opening new opportunities for freelancers and businesses alike. GPT, while not perfect, offers significant assistance in generating accurate translations for a variety of languages, particularly for general content. This summary provides practical tips, examples, and resources to help you maximise your earning potential through text translation services using GPT.

How GPT Can Assist in Text Translation

GPT offers several advantages when it comes to translating text:

- **Quick translations** : GPT can translate content rapidly, allowing you to handle high volumes of work efficiently.
- **Multiple languages** : GPT can translate text into various languages, making it a versatile tool for international markets.
- **Contextual understanding** : Unlike basic machine translation tools, GPT has the ability to understand context better, which can lead to more accurate translations.
- **Tone and style adaptation** : GPT can help ensure that the tone and style of the original text are maintained during translation, making the translated text more natural and suited to its intended audience.

- **Multilingual content generation** : GPT can generate content directly in a foreign language, which can save time when creating multilingual documents.

Practical Tips to Maximise Earnings from Translation Services

1. **Focus on specific language pairs** : Offering translation services in niche or high-demand language pairs, such as English to Mandarin or English to Arabic, can allow you to charge higher rates. Specialising in fewer languages will also help you improve quality and accuracy.
2. **Offer translation and localisation services** : Beyond simple translations, offer localisation services where the content is adapted to the cultural context of the target language. This is particularly important for marketing content, websites, and product descriptions.
3. **Combine AI with human editing** : While GPT can handle most of the initial translation work, human proofreading is often necessary to ensure the translation is culturally appropriate and free from nuances

that AI might miss. This combination allows you to offer higher-quality services.

4. **Price according to complexity** : Simple, straightforward texts can be translated quickly using GPT, allowing you to charge lower rates for quick turnaround times. However, more complex texts, such as legal, technical, or academic documents, should be priced higher due to the additional editing and accuracy checks required.

5. **Utilise post-editing of machine translation (PEMT)** : This is a service where AI tools like GPT provide the initial translation, and you perform thorough editing to ensure the translation is flawless. PEMT services are growing in demand, and you can offer this as a more affordable option for clients compared to manual translation.

6. **Expand into multilingual content creation** : Offer clients a complete service by creating original content in multiple languages, such as blog posts, product descriptions, or marketing materials. This expands your offering beyond translation and makes you more competitive.

Example: Translating Marketing Materials

Suppose you are hired to translate a company's marketing brochure from English to French. Here's how GPT can help:

- **Initial translation** : GPT can quickly translate the brochure, capturing the main ideas and maintaining the persuasive tone.
- **Editing for localisation** : As French marketing terms and cultural preferences may differ from English, you would review and adjust phrases to ensure the content resonates with the French-speaking audience. For instance, sales language might need a softer or more formal tone in French than in English.
- **Final proofreading** : Human review is essential to ensure the translation reads naturally and is free from errors.

By offering localisation alongside translation, you provide added value, making your services more appealing to businesses seeking international expansion.

Resources to Boost Your Translation Business

- **DeepL Translator** : A popular AI-powered translation tool known for its accuracy, especially in European languages. Use it alongside GPT to cross-check translations or improve quality.
- **Google Translate** : Although less nuanced than GPT, it's useful for quick translations or double-checking specific terms or phrases.
- **Smartling** : A cloud-based platform for managing multilingual content. It offers tools for both human and AI-assisted translations, helping you streamline your workflow.
- **SDL Trados Studio** : A popular translation software used by professional translators, particularly for technical and legal documents. It helps maintain consistency and improves efficiency.
- **Freelancing Platforms** : Platforms like ProZ.com, Fiverr, Upwork, and PeoplePerHour are excellent for connecting with clients who need translation services. These platforms also allow you to offer both translation and localisation services.

Maximising Earnings from Translation Services

1. **Charge per word or project** : Pricing translation services by the word is common in the industry. However, for large or complex projects, offering a project-based rate can make your services more competitive while ensuring fair compensation for your time.

2. **Offer multilingual packages** : Provide translation services across multiple languages for businesses expanding into different markets. Bundling these services into packages allows you to charge more and offer greater value to clients.

3. **Focus on high-demand industries** : Certain industries, such as legal, medical, and technical fields, require precise translations and are willing to pay higher rates. Specialising in these fields can help you command premium pricing.

4. **Develop long-term relationships with businesses** : Establish ongoing relationships with companies that frequently require translation services for their websites, product manuals, or customer communications. Offering regular services through retainer agreements can provide a steady stream of income.

5. **Target content creators and self-publishers** : Many self-published authors and content creators want to reach a global audience. Offering affordable translation services for e-books, blogs, or video scripts allows you to tap into this growing market.

Additional Revenue Streams

1. **Content localisation** : Offer localisation services for websites, mobile apps, and software. This involves not only translating text but also adapting visuals, UI elements, and product descriptions for different markets, creating another lucrative income stream.
2. **Subtitling and transcription services** : Translating and subtitling video content or transcribing audio for global audiences is a growing need, particularly in media and education. Offering multilingual subtitling can significantly boost your earnings.
3. **Certified translation services** : Obtaining certification as a translator allows you to provide legal or official document translation, which often commands higher

fees. Certification requirements vary by country but can be a valuable qualification.

4. **Editing machine-generated translations** : As businesses increasingly turn to AI translation tools, there is growing demand for professional editors who can refine and perfect machine-generated translations. By offering this service, you can capitalise on the trend while maintaining human quality.

5. **Create translation glossaries or style guides** : Some businesses may need regular translations with specific terminology. Offering a customised glossary or style guide for their content can create additional value and encourage ongoing partnerships.

Leveraging AI for Efficient Translation

1. **Combine AI with professional software** : While GPT is powerful, combining it with other translation software such as SDL Trados or MemoQ ensures consistency in terminology and style across large projects.

2. **Offer consulting on multilingual strategies** : Many businesses are unfamiliar with the complexities of entering new linguistic markets. Offering consultation

services on how to approach multilingual content strategies, translation workflows, and market preferences adds value and allows you to charge more.

3. **Stay up-to-date with AI advancements** : As AI translation tools evolve, staying informed about new features and tools will give you a competitive edge. Platforms like OpenAI or translation-focused companies frequently release updates that enhance accuracy and usability.

By integrating GPT into your workflow, you can offer faster, high-quality translations while also maintaining the human touch needed for complex projects. With a strategic focus on high-demand industries, specialised language pairs, and comprehensive localisation services, you can maximise your earning potential as a translator in today's global market.

Chapter 17
Summarising Academic Papers

Summarising academic papers is a valuable service in high demand across various sectors, including academia, research, and business. With the complexity of research papers and the need for concise information, offering summarisation services can be highly lucrative. This summary provides practical tips, examples, and resources to help you leverage tools like GPT and maximise your earning potential in this field.

How GPT Can Assist in Summarising Academic Papers

GPT offers several benefits for summarising academic papers, especially when dealing with complex and technical content:

- **Quick summaries** : GPT can generate concise summaries of long papers, helping you save time.
- **Adaptable style** : It can create summaries in different formats, whether you need a detailed summary or a brief abstract.
- **Subject understanding** : GPT can handle technical language, especially in fields like medicine, engineering, and social sciences, making it a useful tool for summarising complex research.
- **Customisable tone** : GPT can generate summaries that match the desired tone, whether it's for an academic audience or a general readership.

Practical Tips to Maximise Earnings from Summarising Academic Papers

1. **Choose a specialisation** : Focusing on specific fields like medicine, law, engineering, or social sciences can help you build a reputation for expertise. Academic subjects often use highly specialised language, and proficiency in a specific area allows you to charge premium rates.
2. **Offer different levels of summarisation** : Provide a range of summarisation services, such as:

   - **Abstract summaries** : Short, concise overviews of the main findings and conclusions.
   - **Executive summaries** : A more detailed summary that includes methodology, key results, and implications.
   - **Detailed breakdowns** : Comprehensive summaries that break down each section of the paper (e.g., introduction, literature review, methods, and findings).

3. **Use GPT as a starting point** : GPT can generate a first draft summary, but you should always refine and edit the output to ensure it accurately captures the research's nuances. This combination of AI and human expertise will provide higher-quality results.
4. **Understand your audience** : Tailor your summaries based on who will read them. For example, a summary for a research funder will focus on the paper's impact and relevance, while a summary for students may need to break down complex concepts into simpler terms.
5. **Stay updated with research trends** : Staying informed about developments in the fields you summarise allows you to offer more insightful and relevant summaries. Regularly reading academic journals helps you understand the context of the papers you work on.

Example: Summarising a Scientific Research Paper

Suppose you are asked to summarise a research paper on climate change for a general audience. Here's how you can approach it:

- **Abstract-level summary** : Provide a concise paragraph highlighting the research question, key findings, and conclusion.
- **Executive summary** : Include the paper's background, the hypothesis being tested, the methods used, the results, and the paper's broader implications.
- **Tailored tone** : If the summary is for policymakers, you might emphasise the practical implications of the findings. For an academic audience, you would include more detail about the methodology and data analysis.

This flexibility allows you to meet diverse client needs, increasing your potential earning opportunities.

Resources to Help with Summarising Academic Papers

- **Google Scholar** : An essential tool for finding and accessing academic papers. It also provides citation data, which can be useful when summarising.

- **Zotero** : A reference management tool that helps you organise academic papers and easily reference sources in your summaries.
- **GPT-3 or GPT-4** : OpenAI's models can be used to generate initial summaries of research papers. Use the summarisation prompt features to extract the key points and findings.
- **JSTOR** : Access to a wide range of academic papers across various disciplines, which can help you familiarise yourself with topics and trends.
- **Mendeley** : Another reference manager that can help you organise research papers and collaborate with other researchers.

Maximising Earnings from Summarisation Services

1. **Charge by word or project** : Pricing per word or per project is common for summarisation services. For instance, you might charge more for longer papers or highly technical content.
2. **Offer tailored summaries for different audiences** : Academic papers often need summarising for various audiences, such as students, researchers, and industry

professionals. Offering bespoke summaries, such as simplifying the content for students or focusing on data analysis for industry experts, can command higher fees.

3. **Expand into academic writing** : In addition to summaries, you can offer related services like literature reviews, research proposals, or academic editing. Expanding your service offering increases your appeal to academic clients and students.

4. **Target academic professionals** : Researchers, professors, and students often need summarised versions of lengthy papers for grant applications, literature reviews, or study purposes. Offering your services to these groups can lead to repeat business, especially for large research projects or ongoing collaborations.

5. **Provide summarisation for businesses** : Many industries, particularly in technology, healthcare, and finance, rely on academic research to inform decision-making. Offering summarisation services to companies allows them to stay informed without having to read lengthy papers themselves. Tailor summaries to focus on actionable insights and industry relevance.

Additional Revenue Streams

1. **Academic consulting** : With expertise in summarising academic research, you can offer consulting services to businesses or institutions seeking advice on research trends and insights. This allows you to charge higher fees for specialised knowledge.
2. **Create academic course materials** : Offering summarised research as part of online courses or educational content creation can be a profitable side business. Researchers and professors may need summaries for course notes or lectures.
3. **Summarising for grant applications** : Researchers often need concise versions of their work to submit in grant applications or project proposals. You can offer a specialised service focused on distilling research into compelling and precise grant submissions.
4. **SEO-based summaries for websites** : Some websites or platforms that discuss academic research, such as blogs or news outlets, need SEO-friendly summaries to attract a broader audience. Offering this service taps into the online content creation market.

5. **Offering workshops or training** : Consider offering workshops or online tutorials on how to effectively summarise academic papers for students or junior researchers. This can generate additional income and position you as an expert in academic summarisation.

Leveraging AI Tools for Summarisation

1. **Refine AI outputs** : GPT can offer a draft summary, but adding human insight ensures the summary is accurate, nuanced, and aligned with the paper's core arguments. This is particularly important for technical or highly specialised content.
2. **Combine AI tools** : Use GPT alongside other AI tools like QuillBot or SummarizeBot, which offer different approaches to summarisation. These tools can complement GPT's work, improving accuracy and diversity in your output.
3. **Use reference management tools** : Using tools like Zotero or Mendeley allows you to efficiently manage and cite papers, which is essential when working with academic material. Proper citations increase the

credibility and professionalism of your summaries.

By offering high-quality academic summaries and tailoring your services to different markets, you can maximise your earning potential. Combining AI tools like GPT with human expertise and providing value-added services such as consulting or grant writing will help you stand out in this competitive field.

Chapter 18
Creating AI-Generated Poetry

AI-generated poetry has emerged as a fascinating blend of technology and creativity, offering poets and creators new ways to produce and market literary works. With tools like GPT, you can generate poems in various styles, lengths, and themes, allowing you to tap into both artistic and commercial opportunities. This summary will provide practical tips, examples, and resources to help you maximise your earning potential through AI-generated poetry.

How GPT Can Assist in Generating Poetry

GPT, a powerful language model, can generate poetry that mimics a wide range of poetic forms and styles, from classic sonnets to free verse. Here are some of its key benefits:

- **Versatility in style** : GPT can create poetry in multiple formats, including haikus, limericks, sonnets, and free verse. It can mimic famous poets' styles or create something entirely original.
- **Speed** : You can quickly generate multiple versions of a poem, helping to brainstorm ideas or refine an existing piece.
- **Adaptability** : GPT can adjust the tone, mood, or subject of the poem based on your prompts, allowing for personalised or themed poetry.

Practical Tips to Maximise Earnings from AI-Generated Poetry

1. **Find a niche** : Identify a specific audience or market for your AI-generated poetry. Some potential niches include greeting cards,

personalised poems for special occasions (birthdays, weddings, anniversaries), or poetry for social media platforms.

2. **Collaborate with artists** : Collaborating with visual artists, musicians, or designers can help you create multimedia art that incorporates AI-generated poetry. This can be used for digital prints, book covers, or music videos, increasing your earning potential through cross-disciplinary projects.

3. **Offer custom poetry** : Use GPT to generate personalised poems for individuals or businesses. Clients may request poems for loved ones, company events, or marketing campaigns, allowing you to charge a premium for unique, tailored content.

4. **Publish AI-generated poetry collections** : Compile AI-generated poems into digital or physical books. You can self-publish through platforms like Amazon Kindle Direct Publishing (KDP), IngramSpark, or Blurb. Offering themed collections, such as love poems, nature poems, or motivational verses, can appeal to specific reader interests.

5. **Leverage social media platforms** : Share AI-generated poems on social media platforms such as Instagram, Twitter, or TikTok. Many creators have built large followings by regularly posting bite-sized

poetic content. Once you gain traction, you can monetise your audience through sponsored posts, merchandise, or poetry books.

6. **Sell poetry NFTs** : Enter the growing world of non-fungible tokens (NFTs) by creating unique AI-generated poems as digital assets. You can sell these poems on NFT platforms like OpenSea, Foundation, or Rarible. Offering limited editions or collaborative NFT art with other creators can add value to your digital poetry pieces.

7. **Create poetry prompts** : Develop and sell curated poetry prompts or inspiration packs for aspiring poets. AI-generated poetry can serve as an example or starting point for creative writing exercises, which can be marketed to writers, teachers, or poetry enthusiasts.

8. **Use AI to assist with traditional poetry** : While GPT can generate entire poems, it's also useful for providing creative inspiration. If you are a poet, you can use AI to assist with writer's block, generate ideas, or provide alternative word choices or line structures.

Example: Personalised Poetry for a Wedding

Suppose a client commissions you to write a personalised wedding poem. Here's how GPT can assist:

- **Initial draft** : Provide GPT with details about the couple's love story, key moments, and special memories. GPT can then generate a draft poem that incorporates these elements.
- **Refinement** : Once you receive the AI-generated poem, you can refine it by editing certain lines, enhancing the emotional impact, or adjusting the style to suit the couple's preferences.
- **Final product** : Offer the poem in various formats, such as a printed piece on custom stationery or as part of a wedding video, adding more value to your service.

This personalised poetry can be sold at a premium and marketed as a unique, heartfelt gift or wedding keepsake.

Resources to Help with AI-Generated Poetry

- **OpenAI GPT-3 or GPT-4** : These language models are key tools for generating poetry. Experiment with different prompts and parameters to fine-tune the style and content of your poems.
- **Sudowrite** : A tool that uses AI to help writers generate creative content. It can assist in creating poetic verses, particularly by suggesting alternative lines or words.
- **Poet's Pad** : A writing app designed for poets that can help you structure poems and find inspiration. Pair it with AI-generated ideas for more creative output.
- **Canva** : A design platform that allows you to create visually appealing layouts for your AI-generated poetry. Use it to design greeting cards, social media posts, or printables.
- **Blurb** : A self-publishing platform where you can create and sell print books or e-books of your AI-generated poetry collections.

Maximising Earnings from AI-Generated Poetry

1. **Charge per poem or package** : Offer AI-generated poems as individual commissions

or in themed bundles. You can create tiered pricing based on the length, complexity, or personalisation required.

2. **Sell poetry in different formats** : Create and sell your poems as posters, digital prints, greeting cards, or even apparel. Online marketplaces like Etsy or Redbubble are ideal for selling these products.

3. **Create a subscription service** : Offer a subscription-based service where customers receive monthly AI-generated poems. You could cater this to specific themes, such as love, inspiration, or seasonal content.

4. **Target different markets** : Expand your services to cater to businesses looking for creative copy, such as unique product descriptions, slogans, or marketing materials infused with poetic language.

5. **Monetise through social media** : By building a following on platforms like Instagram or TikTok, you can monetise your content through brand sponsorships, donations, or selling your work directly to your audience.

Additional Revenue Streams

1. **Poetry workshops and tutorials** : Offer workshops or online courses on AI-assisted poetry writing, where you teach others how to use GPT to enhance their own creative writing. You can sell these courses on platforms like Udemy or Teachable.

2. **Create poetry for brands** : Many brands are exploring creative marketing approaches, and poetry can be a unique way to convey a brand's message. Offer AI-generated poetry as part of brand campaigns, advertisements, or social media content.

3. **Collaborate with influencers** : Partner with influencers or creators in the art, music, or fashion spaces who might be interested in using AI-generated poetry as part of their projects. This can give your poetry wider exposure and open up new revenue streams.

4. **Crowdfunding projects** : Use crowdfunding platforms like Kickstarter or Patreon to fund your AI-generated poetry projects, such as poetry collections or art installations that incorporate your poems.

5. **Sell poetry writing prompts** : AI-generated poetry can serve as inspiration for aspiring

poets. Package and sell creative writing prompts that come with examples of AI-generated poems, which can be used by schools, writing groups, or individual writers.

Leveraging AI for Creative Poetry Generation

1. **Experiment with different prompts** : Play around with specific prompts to see how GPT responds in different poetic styles, forms, and tones. A well-crafted prompt can result in poetry that feels deeply personalised and unique.
2. **Use AI to complement your own creativity** : Rather than relying entirely on AI, use GPT to assist your creative process. Generate rough drafts or alternative lines that you can edit and refine into a final piece.
3. **Stay updated with AI advancements** : AI models continue to evolve, with better understanding of language and creative writing. Stay informed about new features in GPT and other AI tools that might enhance your poetic generation skills.

By using AI to generate poetry, you can tap into a variety of creative and commercial opportunities.

Whether you're crafting custom poems for clients, publishing collections, or collaborating with other artists, AI-generated poetry can expand your creative reach and earning potential.

Chapter 19
Personalised Resume and Cover Letter Writing

Personalised resume and cover letter writing is a valuable service, particularly in today's competitive job market. With AI tools like GPT, you can streamline the process, offering clients tailored documents that help them stand out. By combining human insight with AI capabilities, you can offer high-quality services that appeal to job seekers across various industries. This summary provides practical tips, examples, and resources to help you maximise your earning potential through personalised resume and cover letter writing.

How GPT Can Assist in Resume and Cover Letter Writing

GPT can assist in various aspects of resume and cover letter writing:

- **Customisation** : GPT can generate role-specific content by tailoring resumes and cover letters to match job descriptions, highlighting relevant skills, achievements, and qualifications.
- **Time efficiency** : AI speeds up the writing process by providing drafts that can be quickly edited and refined, saving time when working with multiple clients.
- **Professional tone** : GPT ensures that resumes and cover letters are written with appropriate formality and clarity, helping clients present themselves in the best possible light.

Practical Tips to Maximise Earnings from Resume and Cover Letter Writing

1. **Offer a range of services** : Provide clients with flexible options, such as resume writing, cover letter creation, LinkedIn profile optimisation, and interview coaching. Offering bundled services can increase your overall earnings.
2. **Tailor documents to specific industries** : Clients in different sectors (e.g., finance, tech, healthcare) require resumes and cover

letters that reflect industry-specific language, certifications, and skills. Offering industry-specific expertise will set you apart from generic writing services.

3. **Provide multiple resume formats** : Clients often need resumes in different formats (e.g., chronological, functional, or combination). Offering tailored formatting services can increase the perceived value of your work and attract a wider range of clients.

4. **Create ATS-friendly resumes** : Applicant Tracking Systems (ATS) are used by many companies to filter resumes. Make sure to use keywords and formatting that ensure the document passes these systems. GPT can help generate keyword-rich content, but it's essential to understand how ATS works for optimal results.

5. **Focus on achievements** : Highlight quantifiable achievements rather than simple job responsibilities. GPT can generate lists of skills and responsibilities, but as an expert, you should help clients reframe their work history to show measurable outcomes (e.g., "Increased sales by 20% in Q3").

6. **Offer revisions and feedback** : Offering a round of revisions based on client feedback ensures satisfaction and builds trust.

Positioning yourself as both a writer and a career consultant can allow you to charge more for this personalised service.

Example: Writing a Cover Letter for a Marketing Role

A client applying for a marketing role requests a personalised cover letter. Here's how you can use GPT to assist:

- **Initial draft** : Provide GPT with information about the job description, the client's experience, and skills. The AI can generate a draft that highlights the client's qualifications in a structured, professional manner.
- **Customisation** : Refine the content to focus on the client's specific achievements and how they align with the company's goals. For example, if the job involves digital marketing, emphasise the client's success in running online campaigns or increasing web traffic.
- **Final touches** : Adjust the tone and personalisation to make the letter feel more authentic and less generic. Adding a few specific details about the company or role can make the client stand out.

Resources to Help with Resume and Cover Letter Writing

- **Jobscan** : This tool analyses resumes and cover letters, comparing them to job descriptions to ensure they are ATS-friendly. Use this tool to optimise documents for your clients.
- **LinkedIn** : A key platform for professional networking. Offer clients LinkedIn profile optimisation services as an add-on to your resume and cover letter writing.
- **Canva** : For clients who need visually appealing resumes, Canva allows you to create modern, professional designs that stand out.
- **Resumake** : A free tool to create resume templates quickly. You can use it to offer clients a variety of design options, especially for creative or design-focused roles.
- **Grammarly** : Use this tool to ensure that all documents are grammatically correct and polished before delivering them to clients.

Maximising Earnings from Personalised Resume and Cover Letter Writing

1. **Charge premium rates for personalisation** : Offer clients highly tailored resumes and cover letters based on deep industry knowledge or senior roles. These require more detailed work, allowing you to charge more.
2. **Target specific client demographics** : Focus on niche markets, such as executives, recent graduates, or career changers. Each group has different needs, and offering specialised services (e.g., executive resumes or entry-level cover letters) can set you apart from competitors.
3. **Offer express services** : Clients often need last-minute help. Offering an expedited service for a higher fee can be highly profitable.
4. **Build long-term relationships with clients** : Many job seekers apply to multiple roles. Offering discounted packages or subscriptions for multiple resume and cover letter revisions can generate steady income over time.
5. **Leverage testimonials and case studies** : Successful placements or positive feedback from clients can boost your credibility.

Sharing testimonials or case studies on your website or LinkedIn can help you attract new business.

Additional Revenue Streams

1. **Career coaching services** : Expand your business to include career coaching, interview preparation, or salary negotiation workshops. Many job seekers will pay a premium for these additional services.
2. **Online courses and workshops** : Develop and sell courses or workshops on resume writing, cover letter strategies, and job search techniques. Platforms like Udemy or Skillshare allow you to reach a broad audience and generate passive income.
3. **Collaborate with recruitment agencies** : Partnering with recruitment agencies or headhunters allows you to offer resume and cover letter writing services to their clients, expanding your customer base.
4. **Write for job boards** : Many job search platforms and career websites need content, such as articles or guides on resume writing or job applications. You can generate income by writing for these sites and positioning yourself as an expert.

5. **Monetise blog content** : Start a blog focused on job search tips and resume writing strategies. Over time, you can monetise the blog through advertising, affiliate links, or by offering paid consulting services.

Leveraging AI for Personalised Resume and Cover Letter Writing

1. **Use AI to generate different versions** : GPT can quickly produce multiple versions of a resume or cover letter, each tailored to a different job description. This allows you to offer clients more options and cater to a range of applications.
2. **Pair AI with human expertise** : While GPT can generate content efficiently, you must review and refine the output to ensure accuracy and personalisation. Combining AI's speed with your expertise will deliver high-quality results that meet client needs.
3. **Stay updated on industry trends** : AI is continuously evolving, with new tools and features becoming available. Stay informed about advancements in AI writing tools that can enhance the quality and efficiency of

your resume and cover letter writing services.

By offering personalised, high-quality resume and cover letter writing services, you can tap into a lucrative market of job seekers who need help standing out. Leveraging AI tools like GPT while combining them with your expertise will help you create effective, tailored documents that lead to client success. Diversifying your services, targeting niche markets, and utilising resources like ATS software and design platforms will further maximise your earning potential.

Chapter 20
Developing Business Plans

Developing business plans is a crucial service for entrepreneurs, startups, and established companies looking to secure investment, launch new ventures, or expand operations. By leveraging AI tools like GPT, you can efficiently craft comprehensive, structured business plans that meet clients' unique needs. This summary provides practical tips, examples, and resources to help you maximise your earning potential through developing business plans.

How GPT Can Assist in Business Plan Development

GPT can significantly streamline the process of creating business plans by generating content that covers key sections, such as market analysis, business models, and financial forecasts. Here are some ways it can assist:

- **Content generation** : GPT can quickly draft sections of a business plan, including executive summaries, company overviews, and marketing strategies. It ensures consistency in tone and style, while saving time in the writing process.
- **Customisation** : GPT can tailor business plans to specific industries, markets, or business types, helping you create personalised plans that meet the needs of your clients.
- **Idea development** : For entrepreneurs unsure of how to articulate their ideas, GPT can help generate clear and concise descriptions of their business concepts, objectives, and goals.

Practical Tips to Maximise Earnings from Business Plan Development

1. **Offer tailored business plans** : Each business has unique needs. Offer plans customised for different purposes, such as startup funding, internal strategy, or franchising, and charge accordingly. Tailoring a business plan to specific sectors (e.g., tech, retail, or hospitality) can also justify higher fees.
2. **Incorporate visual elements** : Investors and stakeholders often appreciate visual representations of data. Use charts, graphs, and financial projections to enhance the professionalism of the plan. Tools like Canva or Microsoft Excel can help with this.
3. **Focus on financial projections** : Detailed financial forecasts are a critical part of any business plan. While GPT can draft narratives, you'll need to create financial models manually. Offering comprehensive financial projections, including income statements, cash flow forecasts, and break-even analyses, can increase the value of your service.
4. **Provide market analysis** : GPT can assist in drafting general market trends, but you should offer detailed and customised market

research. Using reliable sources like Statista, IBISWorld, or government databases to back up your insights will add credibility to the business plan.

5. **Offer revisions and updates** : Business plans often need to be revised or updated over time. Offering clients a revision service or an annual review can provide recurring income while helping clients adapt to changing market conditions.

6. **Create an executive summary service** : Some clients may only need a high-level overview to present to investors. By offering a separate service to create concise, compelling executive summaries, you can tap into this niche market.

Example: Creating a Business Plan for a Tech Startup

Suppose a tech startup approaches you to create a business plan aimed at securing venture capital. Here's how GPT can assist:

- **Initial draft** : GPT can generate an outline covering key sections like the problem the startup is solving, the solution, market opportunity, and revenue model. It can also draft parts of the executive summary and business description.

- **Market analysis** : While GPT can provide a general framework, you'll need to research specific trends, competitors, and potential customer segments to add depth and authority to the market analysis section.
- **Financial projections** : Create detailed financial models based on the startup's projected sales, costs, and growth trajectory. Incorporate charts and graphs to visually represent key financial data.
- **Final touches** : Edit and refine the plan to ensure that it is tailored to the startup's goals, investor expectations, and industry standards.

Resources to Help with Business Plan Development

- **LivePlan** : A popular business plan software that offers templates, financial forecasting tools, and industry benchmarks. It helps create professional, investor-ready business plans.
- **Canva** : For creating visually appealing charts, graphs, and design elements within your business plans. Canva's easy-to-use

interface allows you to add custom graphics to enhance your presentation.

- **Statista** : A data platform that provides detailed market research and industry reports. Use it for accurate data to back up market analysis in business plans.
- **IBISWorld** : Another excellent resource for market research, offering in-depth reports on various industries and sectors.
- **Google Trends** : Useful for identifying market trends and consumer interests. It can be used to enhance the market analysis section of your business plans.

Maximising Earnings from Business Plan Development

1. **Charge premium rates for investor-ready plans** : Business plans that are designed to attract investment require a higher level of detail, especially in financial forecasting and market analysis. Charge premium rates for these plans, as they often involve more work and expert input.
2. **Offer industry-specific plans** : Specialising in a particular industry (e.g., healthcare, technology, or retail) allows you to offer more value by understanding the unique

challenges and opportunities in that sector. Clients are willing to pay more for industry-specific expertise.

3. **Provide additional consulting services** : Position yourself as a business consultant rather than just a plan writer. Offer strategic advice on business growth, market entry, or scaling. By offering these services, you can charge more for your expertise.
4. **Create template packages** : Some entrepreneurs may not need a full business plan service but could benefit from a high-quality template. Sell industry-specific business plan templates with optional customisation as an additional revenue stream.
5. **Expand into pitch decks** : Many startups and businesses need both a business plan and a pitch deck to present to investors. Offering both services as a package allows you to charge a higher rate while providing clients with a complete fundraising toolkit.

Additional Revenue Streams

1. **Business plan workshops** : Offer workshops or online courses teaching entrepreneurs how to develop their own

business plans. Platforms like Udemy, Teachable, or Skillshare are ideal for selling these courses.

2. **Collaborate with accountants and lawyers** : Partner with professionals who offer related services. Accountants can assist with financial projections, and lawyers can review legal aspects, making your business plans more comprehensive.

3. **Pitch deck creation** : Investors often request pitch decks along with business plans. Expand your services to include the creation of professional, visually appealing pitch decks that summarise key business plan elements.

4. **Subscription service for startups** : Offer a subscription model where you provide ongoing support and updates for business plans, financial models, or market research. This can ensure long-term client relationships and recurring revenue.

5. **Business coaching** : Complement your business plan services with coaching on business strategy, scaling operations, or preparing for investor meetings. Many clients will pay extra for ongoing advice and support.

Leveraging AI for Business Plan Development

1. **Generate drafts quickly** : GPT can help you create the initial draft of key sections such as the executive summary, business description, and marketing strategy. This saves time, allowing you to focus on refining the more complex parts of the plan, such as financial projections.

2. **Use AI to assist with market research** : GPT can provide summaries of general market trends, which you can then supplement with more detailed, specific data from research tools like Statista or IBISWorld.

3. **Tailor AI-generated content** : While GPT provides a good starting point, you'll need to customise the content to meet client-specific needs. Focus on making the language clear, persuasive, and aligned with the business's goals and industry.

4. **Stay updated on AI advancements** : As AI tools continue to evolve, new features may become available to enhance the quality and efficiency of business plan development. Stay informed about these advancements to keep your services competitive.

By offering high-quality, customised business plans, you can tap into a lucrative market of entrepreneurs, startups, and established businesses. Leveraging AI tools like GPT will allow you to streamline content generation while focusing on delivering value in key areas such as financial projections and market research. Diversifying your services and expanding into related areas like pitch decks, consulting, and workshops will further maximise your earning potential.

Chapter 21
Writing White Papers and Reports

Writing white papers and reports is a highly valuable service in industries that require detailed, authoritative documents to communicate complex information. White papers are often used in B2B marketing, government, and tech industries to explain products, services, or research findings in a persuasive and informative way. Reports, on the other hand, provide factual data or findings, often used in academic, business, and technical fields. This summary provides practical tips, examples, and resources to help you maximise your earning potential through writing white papers and reports.

How GPT Can Assist in Writing White Papers and Reports

GPT can be a powerful tool to assist in writing both white papers and reports:

- **Initial drafts** : GPT can generate well-structured drafts based on prompts that outline key concepts, helping you save time during the initial writing stage.
- **Complex explanations** : GPT can explain complex ideas clearly, aiding in crafting sections that require detailed descriptions of technologies, methodologies, or processes.
- **Research assistance** : While GPT can't replace human research, it can help summarise findings from source material and generate content based on those summaries, assisting in creating detailed literature reviews or industry analysis sections.

Practical Tips to Maximise Earnings from Writing White Papers and Reports

1. **Offer industry-specific expertise** : Clients value expertise. Specialising in industries such as technology, finance, healthcare, or energy allows you to charge more for your in-depth knowledge. Focus on sectors where white papers and reports are frequently required.

2. **Provide data-driven content** : Use reliable data and research to back up claims in your white papers and reports. Whether you're working with industry statistics or academic research, ensure that your work is credible and supported by factual data.

3. **Tailor for specific audiences** : White papers often need to be written for decision-makers, while reports might be more technical or focused on presenting research findings. Always ensure your writing is tailored to the intended audience, whether it's C-level executives or academic peers.

4. **Focus on structure and clarity** : Both white papers and reports should be well-organised. A clear structure, including sections like an introduction, background, problem statement, solution (in white papers), or methodology and results (in

reports), will make your work more impactful and easier for readers to navigate.

5. **Incorporate visual elements** : Add graphs, charts, and tables to illustrate data. Visual elements not only break up the text but also make the document more engaging. Tools like Canva or Excel can help create professional visuals.

6. **Offer revisions and updates** : Clients may require updated versions of white papers or reports as new data or research becomes available. Offering a service for regular updates can lead to recurring income.

Example: Writing a White Paper on Cybersecurity Solutions

If you're tasked with writing a white paper on cybersecurity solutions for a tech firm, GPT can help in the following ways:

- **Drafting the problem and solution** : GPT can outline the challenges businesses face with cybersecurity threats and propose solutions using the company's technology or services.
- **Market analysis** : With your input, GPT can generate a summary of industry trends and

risks, although detailed research will need to be sourced separately.

- **Finalisation** : You would then refine the draft by adding case studies, real-world examples, and specific data that highlights the company's expertise and value proposition.

Resources to Help with Writing White Papers and Reports

- **Google Scholar** : A valuable resource for accessing peer-reviewed academic papers and credible sources for research.
- **Statista** : This platform provides a wealth of data and statistics across industries that you can incorporate into your white papers or reports to back up claims.
- **Mendeley** : A reference management tool that helps organise research and citations, making it easier to compile thorough and well-cited reports.
- **Canva** : Use Canva to create professional visual elements like graphs, charts, and infographics to include in your white papers and reports.
- **Grammarly** : This tool can help with proofreading and ensuring your white paper

or report is free from grammatical errors and maintains a formal tone.

Maximising Earnings from Writing White Papers and Reports

1. **Charge premium rates for detailed research** : White papers and reports often require deep research and data analysis. Charge higher rates for documents that need extensive investigation, interviews, or data gathering.
2. **Offer industry insights** : Clients value thought leadership. By positioning yourself as an expert in a specific industry, you can offer premium services that provide not only writing but also strategic advice on content development.
3. **Develop long-term relationships with companies** : Many businesses require white papers or reports on a regular basis, especially in sectors like technology, healthcare, and finance. Building long-term relationships with companies can ensure consistent projects and income.
4. **Expand into related services** : Offer additional services like creating summaries of white papers, executive reports, or

presentations. Many clients need condensed versions of reports for different audiences, allowing you to add value with little extra effort.

5. **Offer quick turnaround services** : Many clients need white papers or reports on short notice. If you can offer expedited services, you can charge premium fees for fast delivery while still maintaining quality.

Additional Revenue Streams

1. **Develop content for marketing campaigns** : White papers are often used as lead generation tools in B2B marketing. Offer clients additional services, such as writing accompanying blog posts, social media content, or landing pages to promote the white paper.

2. **Create report templates** : Some clients may prefer to write their own reports but need templates. Sell professionally designed templates with pre-set structures for white papers and reports, especially for industries with common formats (e.g., annual reports).

3. **Offer editing services** : Some businesses or academics may write their own content

but need help editing or polishing it. Offering proofreading and editorial reviews of white papers and reports can provide an additional income stream.

4. **Teach workshops** : Conduct workshops or online courses on how to write effective white papers and reports. This could be targeted at entrepreneurs, marketers, or students who need to develop these skills for their careers.

5. **Ghostwriting** : Offer ghostwriting services for thought leaders or companies that want to produce white papers under their own name but don't have the time or expertise to write them. Many companies are willing to pay well for this kind of behind-the-scenes service.

Leveraging AI for White Paper and Report Writing

1. **Use AI to create outlines and drafts** : GPT can be particularly useful in generating a clear, organised structure for your white paper or report. Once you have a framework, the AI can also help fill in sections based on your research notes.

2. **Generate summaries** : Many reports and white papers include executive summaries

or conclusions. GPT can assist in summarising long sections of text, helping you produce concise overviews quickly.

3. **Enhance research** : While GPT cannot conduct original research, it can help in summarising and synthesising complex research papers or data, making it easier for you to compile literature reviews or background sections.

4. **Focus on quality control** : While GPT can assist in content creation, always review and edit its output to ensure accuracy, coherence, and that it aligns with your client's needs.

By offering white paper and report writing services, you can tap into a high-value market, particularly in industries where authoritative and detailed documents are essential. Using AI tools like GPT will help streamline content creation, allowing you to focus on research and expert input. By specialising in certain industries, offering tailored solutions, and expanding into related services, you can significantly increase your earning potential.

Chapter 22
Generating Customer Support Responses

Customer support responses are vital in maintaining a positive relationship between businesses and their customers. With the increasing demand for quick, accurate, and professional customer service, AI tools like GPT can assist in generating responses efficiently. This summary outlines practical tips, examples, and resources to help you maximise your earning potential through generating customer support responses.

How GPT Can Assist in Generating Customer Support Responses

GPT can streamline the customer support process by:

- **Automating responses** : GPT can quickly generate responses for common customer queries, saving time for customer service teams.
- **Personalisation** : While GPT provides a template, responses can be tailored to each customer's specific needs, making the communication more personal and effective.
- **Handling various topics** : GPT can generate responses for a wide range of

topics, from product queries to troubleshooting, returns, and feedback.

Practical Tips to Maximise Earnings from Generating Customer Support Responses

1. **Offer customised response templates** : Provide businesses with tailored templates for different types of customer interactions (e.g., complaints, product queries, returns). These templates can be created for specific industries or businesses, increasing the value of your service.
2. **Develop multilingual support** : Offering multilingual customer support responses allows businesses to cater to global audiences. By using GPT's language capabilities, you can create responses in various languages, making your service more valuable.
3. **Set up automation workflows** : Help businesses integrate AI-generated responses into their CRM or customer support platforms (e.g., Zendesk, Freshdesk). This automation improves efficiency and adds value to your offering.
4. **Provide error handling** : Ensure that responses generated by GPT include

guidelines for handling errors or misunderstandings. This prevents potential issues from escalating and maintains a positive customer experience.

5. **Create escalation protocols** : While GPT can handle routine queries, more complex issues may require human intervention. Develop response templates that include clear escalation paths for customers needing further assistance.

Example: Automating Customer Support for an E-commerce Company

Suppose you're tasked with generating customer support responses for an online retail company. GPT can help in the following ways:

- **Order queries** : Generate quick responses for questions about order status, shipping times, or delays, using data from the company's order system to personalise the response.
- **Product issues** : Provide pre-drafted troubleshooting steps for common product problems, helping customers resolve issues without needing to contact a human agent.

- **Return requests** : Create automated responses that guide customers through the returns process, including links to return forms or instructions on packaging.

Resources to Help with Generating Customer Support Responses

- **Zendesk** : A popular customer service platform that allows businesses to integrate AI-generated responses for seamless customer support.
- **Freshdesk** : Another customer support platform that supports AI integration for generating automated responses.
- **Google Translate** : While GPT can generate responses in various languages, tools like Google Translate can assist in fine-tuning translations for multilingual customer support.
- **Grammarly** : Useful for proofreading and ensuring that all responses are grammatically correct and professional in tone.

Maximising Earnings from Generating Customer Support Responses

1. **Offer subscription-based services** : Set up ongoing support for businesses by offering monthly or yearly subscriptions for AI-generated response services. This ensures continuous updates and monitoring of the system's effectiveness.
2. **Target small to medium-sized businesses (SMBs)** : SMBs often need cost-effective customer support solutions. Offer AI-generated responses as a budget-friendly alternative to hiring a large customer service team.
3. **Expand into chatbot creation** : Combine GPT's customer support responses with chatbot technology to create a fully automated customer service experience. Chatbots are in high demand and can significantly increase your revenue.
4. **Offer consulting services** : Help businesses optimise their customer service workflows by integrating AI-generated responses. Position yourself as a customer service consultant who can both implement and refine their support strategies.
5. **Provide ongoing updates** : Offer clients regular updates to their response templates

based on new product releases, changes in customer feedback, or new company policies. This adds value and helps maintain long-term relationships.

Additional Revenue Streams

1. **Develop industry-specific solutions** : Some industries, such as tech support or financial services, require highly specialised customer support. By focusing on these industries, you can offer tailored responses that meet the unique needs of those sectors.
2. **Create a knowledge base** : Offer businesses a full library of AI-generated responses that can be used for FAQs, self-help guides, and troubleshooting. This can be sold as a standalone product or bundled with customer support services.
3. **Offer training services** : Train customer support teams on how to use AI-generated responses effectively. This helps businesses maximise the potential of AI, ensuring high customer satisfaction.
4. **Integrate with live chat platforms** : Many businesses use live chat features to communicate with customers. Offering AI-generated responses that integrate

seamlessly into these platforms can be a highly valuable service.

Leveraging AI for Customer Support Responses

1. **Automate FAQs and common issues** : GPT can quickly handle frequently asked questions (FAQs) or recurring issues like order tracking, product details, and returns. Automating these responses saves time and improves efficiency.
2. **Enhance personalisation** : Use GPT to generate personalised responses by integrating customer data (e.g., name, previous purchases, order number). This makes the interaction feel more personal, even though it's automated.
3. **Train AI models with specific data** : To improve accuracy, GPT can be fine-tuned using data from the client's previous customer interactions, allowing for better contextual understanding and more relevant responses.
4. **Review and edit AI-generated responses** : While GPT can generate responses, it's important to review and edit these to ensure accuracy, tone, and compliance with the company's customer service standards.

By offering AI-generated customer support responses, you can tap into a rapidly growing market where businesses are seeking efficient and cost-effective solutions to enhance their customer service operations. Leveraging GPT for automation, personalisation, and multilingual support, while expanding into consulting, chatbot creation, and industry-specific services, can significantly boost your earning potential.

Chapter 23
Automated Chatbot Creation

Automated chatbots are increasingly becoming essential tools for businesses, allowing them to handle customer queries efficiently, provide round-the-clock support, and enhance customer engagement without the need for constant human intervention. With AI-powered models like GPT, you can create highly functional, responsive, and personalised chatbots that meet a range of customer service needs. This summary provides practical tips, examples, and resources to help you maximise your earning potential through automated chatbot creation.

How GPT Can Assist in Chatbot Creation

GPT can play a pivotal role in chatbot creation by:

- **Generating human-like responses** : Chatbots powered by GPT can engage in natural, conversational exchanges with users, mimicking human interaction and offering seamless support.
- **Handling a wide range of queries** : GPT can manage common customer service inquiries, troubleshooting, FAQs, and even more complex requests across various industries.
- **Customising dialogue** : Responses can be tailored based on the specific requirements of the business, ensuring the chatbot aligns with the company's brand voice and customer expectations.

Practical Tips to Maximise Earnings from Automated Chatbot Creation

1. **Target different industries** : Chatbots are highly adaptable across industries such as e-commerce, healthcare, banking, and

hospitality. Specialising in chatbot creation for a specific industry can help you develop expertise and charge premium prices.

2. **Offer ongoing chatbot training** : Chatbots require updates and maintenance to remain relevant and effective. Offer a service for ongoing training and improvement, fine-tuning the AI model based on real-world customer interactions.

3. **Develop multi-platform chatbots** : Businesses often need chatbots for various platforms, such as websites, social media channels (Facebook Messenger, WhatsApp), and apps. Expanding your services to cover multiple platforms increases your value.

4. **Focus on user experience (UX)** : Ensure the chatbot offers a smooth and intuitive experience, with clear prompts and easy navigation for users. Consider including features such as buttons, quick replies, and menus to enhance usability.

5. **Create escalation paths** : Not all customer queries can be handled by chatbots. Implement escalation protocols where the chatbot can transfer the conversation to a human representative when needed, ensuring complex issues are dealt with properly.

Example: Creating a Chatbot for an E-commerce Business

Imagine building a chatbot for an e-commerce business that handles customer queries related to orders, shipping, and returns:

- **Order tracking** : The chatbot could pull real-time data from the store's backend to provide customers with order status updates.
- **Product recommendations** : By integrating GPT's conversational capabilities, the chatbot can recommend products based on user preferences or previous purchases.
- **Returns and refunds** : The chatbot could walk customers through the returns process, providing links to necessary forms and guidelines on packaging.

Resources to Help with Automated Chatbot Creation

- **Dialogflow by Google** : A powerful tool for creating conversational chatbots with AI capabilities, supporting integration with various platforms.

- **Microsoft Bot Framework** : A comprehensive platform that helps developers build, test, and deploy intelligent bots across multiple channels, including websites, social media, and apps.
- **ManyChat** : A popular tool for building chatbots for platforms like Facebook Messenger and WhatsApp, ideal for marketing and customer engagement.
- **Tars** : A platform for building no-code chatbots that are highly customisable for different industries and use cases.
- **Zapier** : Integrates chatbots with other apps, automating workflows and enabling bots to pull data from CRM systems, email platforms, and other business tools.

Maximising Earnings from Automated Chatbot Creation

1. **Offer full chatbot development packages** : Provide end-to-end services, including design, development, testing, and deployment. Full-service packages allow you to charge higher fees.
2. **Provide chatbot analytics** : Offer insights into chatbot performance, tracking metrics

such as engagement rates, customer satisfaction, and areas for improvement. Analysing this data can lead to additional optimisation services.

3. **Create industry-specific chatbots** : Develop chatbots for industries that rely on customer engagement, such as travel agencies (booking assistance), healthcare (appointment scheduling), or banking (account queries).

4. **Expand into voice-enabled chatbots** : With the rise of voice assistants like Alexa and Google Assistant, voice-enabled chatbots are growing in demand. Offer services for creating voice-activated bots, further diversifying your revenue streams.

5. **Upsell AI integration services** : Help businesses integrate chatbots with other AI tools, such as sentiment analysis or predictive analytics, to provide deeper customer insights and enhanced personalisation.

Additional Revenue Streams

1. **Chatbot templates** : Develop industry-specific chatbot templates that businesses can customise and use. These could be sold

as standalone products for companies that prefer to DIY their chatbot setup.

2. **Subscription-based services** : Offer chatbot maintenance and updates as a subscription service. This ensures the chatbot remains effective and up-to-date with the latest trends and user queries.

3. **Chatbot marketing services** : Create chatbots designed specifically for lead generation and marketing. Many businesses seek bots that can engage customers with promotions, answer product questions, and drive conversions.

4. **White-label chatbot services** : Offer your chatbot creation services as a white-label solution, allowing businesses to rebrand the chatbot as their own. This is particularly appealing to agencies or third-party service providers.

5. **Consulting services** : Help businesses understand the benefits of chatbots and how to implement them effectively. Offer consultancy to guide companies on how best to integrate chatbots into their customer service workflows.

Leveraging AI for Automated Chatbot Creation

1. **Quickly generate responses** : GPT allows you to develop a large library of responses that can be used across different customer scenarios, speeding up chatbot development.
2. **Customise conversation flows** : AI can assist in creating more dynamic and natural conversation flows, moving away from rigid, script-like interactions to more personalised exchanges based on user input.
3. **Multilingual capabilities** : Use GPT to develop chatbots that can respond in multiple languages, making them ideal for businesses with global customer bases.
4. **Incorporate learning mechanisms** : By integrating machine learning models, chatbots can continuously improve over time by learning from user interactions, enabling them to provide better responses and handle more complex queries.

By offering automated chatbot creation, you can tap into a market where businesses seek to improve their customer service and marketing efficiency. GPT provides a solid foundation for generating intelligent, responsive, and customisable chatbots, and by offering a range of additional services such as consultancy, analytics, and white-label solutions, you can significantly boost your earning potential.

Chapter 24
Offering AI-Powered Tutoring Services

AI-powered tutoring services are revolutionising the education sector, offering personalised learning experiences and scalable solutions for students of all ages. Leveraging AI models like GPT, you can create virtual tutoring services that adapt to individual learning needs, provide instant feedback, and offer round-the-clock support. This summary outlines practical tips, examples, and resources to help you maximise your earning potential in offering AI-powered tutoring services.

How AI-Powered Tutoring Services Work

AI tutoring services use advanced natural language processing (NLP) models like GPT to:

- **Deliver personalised learning experiences** : AI can tailor lessons to meet the specific needs and learning pace of each student, offering differentiated support in subjects such as maths, science, or language arts.

- **Provide instant feedback** : Students can receive immediate feedback on their work, improving understanding and retention.
- **Offer flexible learning** : AI tutors are available 24/7, allowing students to learn at their own convenience.
- **Support various subjects** : AI-powered tutors can handle a wide range of subjects and levels, from primary education to university-level courses.

Practical Tips to Maximise Earnings from AI-Powered Tutoring Services

1. **Identify your niche** : Focus on a specific subject area or demographic, such as primary school maths, university-level essay writing, or adult language learning. Specialising can help you stand out in a crowded market and attract a targeted audience.
2. **Offer subscription plans** : Provide tiered subscription plans, where students or parents can choose from different levels of

access, such as basic tutoring, homework help, or one-on-one sessions with human oversight.

3. **Provide assessments and progress tracking** : Create a system where students can take regular assessments, and offer progress reports to parents or educators. This adds value and can justify premium pricing.

4. **Focus on interactive learning** : AI-powered tutoring should be engaging and interactive. Offer quizzes, problem-solving exercises, and interactive lessons to keep students motivated and enhance their learning experience.

5. **Integrate human support** : For complex topics or when students need extra help, offer human tutor oversight. Blending AI and human expertise increases the quality of service and allows for more personalised support.

Example: AI-Powered Maths Tutoring for Secondary School Students

Imagine creating an AI-powered tutoring service specifically designed for secondary school maths:

- **Adaptive lessons** : The AI tutor adapts its teaching style based on the student's strengths and weaknesses, offering more practice in areas where the student struggles and advancing quickly through topics they grasp well.
- **Step-by-step solutions** : The tutor provides detailed, step-by-step solutions for complex problems, allowing students to understand the underlying concepts and not just the answers.
- **Exam preparation** : The AI tutor could generate practice exams and offer tips on test-taking strategies based on the student's performance in prior lessons.

Resources to Help with AI-Powered Tutoring Services

- **Khan Academy** : A well-known platform offering free educational resources that can serve as inspiration for AI-powered tutoring services.
- **Edmodo** : A classroom management tool that allows educators to integrate AI and other technologies into their teaching.
- **Quizlet** : A tool that allows users to create quizzes and study sets. AI-powered tutors

can use similar platforms to create interactive learning experiences.

- **OpenAI GPT** : Utilise GPT to generate lessons, quizzes, and explanations in various subjects, adapting them to different learning levels.
- **Duolingo** : A language-learning app that incorporates AI to personalise lessons, offering a model for how AI-powered tutoring services can engage learners.

Maximising Earnings from AI-Powered Tutoring Services

1. **Offer customised learning plans** : Create tailored learning plans for students based on their initial assessments, offering a premium service for those seeking personalised tutoring.
2. **Expand into different subjects** : Once you've established a successful AI-powered tutoring service in one subject, expand into other areas such as science, history, or language arts, broadening your customer base.
3. **Develop group tutoring options** : Provide group sessions where students can interact with AI tutors and peers. Group tutoring can

be offered at a lower price point while still generating substantial revenue due to the larger number of students involved.

4. **Collaborate with schools and institutions** : Partner with schools, universities, or tutoring centres to integrate your AI-powered tutoring services into their existing educational frameworks. Institutional contracts can provide a steady revenue stream.

5. **Offer multi-language support** : Leverage AI's natural language capabilities to provide tutoring services in multiple languages, catering to international students or those learning new languages.

Additional Revenue Streams

1. **Test preparation services** : Offer AI-powered tutoring specifically for test preparation, such as GCSE, A-levels, SATs, or university entrance exams. Specialised exam preparation can attract students willing to pay higher fees for focused tutoring.

2. **Certification courses** : Develop certification courses in areas like coding, finance, or other specialised skills. Offer certification

upon completion, which can justify a higher price and attract professionals seeking additional qualifications.

3. **Mobile app development** : Create a mobile app version of your AI-powered tutoring service to reach more students and offer a more convenient, on-the-go learning experience.

4. **Online course creation** : Package AI-generated tutoring content into online courses that students can purchase and access at their convenience. These courses can provide passive income once created.

5. **Corporate training** : Offer AI-powered tutoring services to businesses for employee training in specific skills, such as languages, IT, or customer service. This opens up a lucrative B2B revenue stream.

Leveraging AI for Tutoring

1. **Personalise learning** : Use AI to customise lessons based on individual student performance. This allows for tailored support that adapts to the pace and progress of each learner.

2. **Provide real-time feedback** : GPT can generate immediate feedback on

assignments or quizzes, giving students the opportunity to correct mistakes and improve their understanding on the spot.

3. **Improve accessibility** : AI tutors can offer support in multiple languages and for students with different learning needs, making education more accessible to a broader audience.

4. **Continuously improve** : AI-powered tutors can learn from interactions with students, improving their responses and teaching methods over time to provide an even better learning experience.

5. **Integrate multimedia content** : AI tutoring services can incorporate videos, interactive simulations, and other multimedia elements to create a richer, more engaging learning environment.

Maximising Success with AI-Powered Tutoring

- **Offer personalised progress reports** : Parents and educators appreciate data-driven insights into student performance. Providing detailed reports on student progress can add value to your tutoring service.

- **Focus on engagement** : Keep lessons engaging with interactive activities and quizzes that challenge students and keep them motivated to learn.
- **Promote the service on social media** : Build a strong online presence by sharing success stories, student achievements, and engaging content about the benefits of AI-powered learning.

By offering AI-powered tutoring services, you can capitalise on the growing demand for personalised, flexible, and affordable education. With the right blend of adaptive learning, interactivity, and human oversight, you can create a high-value service that meets the needs of students and educators alike while maximising your earning potential.

Chapter 25
Developing Personalised Learning Plans

Creating personalised learning plans (PLPs) is a highly effective way to offer tailored educational experiences that meet the unique needs of individual learners. By using AI-driven tools such as GPT, you can develop adaptive learning programmes that cater to different abilities, learning styles, and goals. Personalised learning plans are valuable in academic tutoring, professional development, and even self-paced learning scenarios. This summary provides practical tips, examples, and resources to help you maximise your earning potential by offering personalised learning plan services.

Benefits of Personalised Learning Plans

Personalised learning plans allow for:

- **Tailored education** : Each plan is customised to fit a learner's strengths, weaknesses, interests, and goals.
- **Improved engagement** : Personalisation helps keep learners motivated by addressing their specific needs and providing relevant content.
- **Flexible pacing** : Learners can progress at their own speed, ensuring they master topics before moving on.
- **Better outcomes** : Personalised learning often leads to higher achievement and retention rates, as it aligns more closely with the learner's natural learning process.

Practical Tips to Maximise Earnings from Personalised Learning Plans

1. **Narrow your niche** : Specialise in a subject or demographic, such as primary school literacy, secondary-level maths, adult career training, or professional certification. Focusing on a niche allows you to charge premium prices for expertise.
2. **Use assessments to build plans** : Start by administering a diagnostic test or assessment to understand the learner's current level, strengths, and areas for improvement. This helps in creating a truly customised learning plan.
3. **Incorporate AI for adaptive learning** : Use AI tools like GPT to generate content dynamically based on the learner's progress, adjusting the learning plan as they advance through lessons.
4. **Offer ongoing support and revisions** : Provide continuous updates and feedback to keep the learning plan relevant and effective. As learners improve or face new challenges, you can adjust their plans accordingly.
5. **Bundle services** : Combine personalised learning plans with tutoring sessions,

progress reports, or exam preparation to offer a full-service educational package.

Example: Personalised Learning Plans for Adult Language Learners

Consider creating personalised learning plans for adults learning English as a second language (ESL):

- **Diagnostic assessment** : Start with an assessment of the learner's current language abilities, focusing on grammar, vocabulary, and pronunciation.
- **Custom content** : Generate lessons that focus on the specific areas where the learner needs improvement, such as conversational skills or business English.
- **Interactive practice** : Include quizzes, speaking exercises, and interactive tasks that align with real-life scenarios relevant to the learner's goals, such as workplace communication or travel.

Resources to Help with Personalised Learning Plans

- **EdTech platforms** : Tools like **Khan Academy**, **Coursera**, and **edX** offer a variety of resources to create and support personalised learning plans.
- **Google Classroom** : A free platform that allows for customised lesson plans, assignments, and progress tracking, ideal for educators creating personal learning environments.
- **LearnDash** : A WordPress plugin designed for creating online courses that can be customised to fit individual learner needs, offering quizzes, assignments, and progress tracking.
- **OpenAI GPT** : Use GPT to generate tailored educational content, exercises, and lessons that adapt to the learner's pace and proficiency.
- **Quizlet** : Create flashcards, quizzes, and other study aids that fit within a personalised learning plan, making it easy for learners to review and retain information.

Maximising Earnings from Personalised Learning Plans

1. **Offer tailored subscription services** : Provide subscription-based personalised learning plans where learners receive continuous updates and new materials as they progress. This model can generate steady, recurring income.
2. **Collaborate with institutions** : Partner with schools, universities, or businesses to offer customised learning plans for their students or employees. Institutional contracts can provide long-term, high-value revenue streams.
3. **Create online courses** : Develop personalised online courses for learners in niche areas, such as coding bootcamps, language proficiency, or exam preparation. These courses can be sold as packages or subscriptions.
4. **Focus on progress tracking** : Offer progress reports and data-driven insights to learners or their parents, demonstrating how the personalised learning plan is helping them achieve their goals.
5. **Bundle with other services** : Combine learning plans with other offerings like tutoring, coaching, or group classes to

create a comprehensive learning experience that justifies a higher price.

Additional Revenue Streams

1. **Corporate training programmes** : Offer personalised learning plans for employee training in areas such as leadership development, IT skills, or communication. Many businesses seek customised training solutions for their staff.
2. **School partnerships** : Work with schools to create personalised plans for students who need extra support or accelerated learning, particularly for students with special educational needs (SEN).
3. **Group learning plans** : While most personalised learning plans are designed for individuals, you can also offer semi-personalised group plans for learners at similar skill levels, helping you scale your services.
4. **Educational consulting** : Provide consultancy services to institutions, helping them implement personalised learning strategies within their curriculum or training programmes.

5. **Certification and accreditation** : Develop personalised plans that help learners achieve professional certifications, offering a clear path to qualification in fields such as IT, finance, or healthcare.

Leveraging AI for Personalised Learning Plans

1. **Content generation** : Use AI to generate dynamic, tailored lessons and exercises that adapt to the learner's progress and challenges.
2. **Real-time feedback** : Offer instant feedback on assignments, quizzes, and practice tasks, allowing learners to correct mistakes and improve understanding quickly.
3. **Adaptive learning paths** : AI can continuously adjust the learning path based on the learner's performance, offering more practice in areas where they struggle and advancing in areas where they excel.
4. **Multilingual support** : Use AI to create learning plans in multiple languages, making your services accessible to a global audience.
5. **Gamification** : Incorporate gamified elements into the learning plan, such as

badges, rewards, and leaderboards, to increase engagement and motivation.

Maximising Success with Personalised Learning Plans

- **Provide ongoing updates** : As the learner progresses, ensure the plan evolves with them. Offer revisions to the learning plan based on their changing needs and goals.
- **Engage learners with varied content** : Keep lessons engaging by incorporating a variety of learning formats, such as videos, interactive exercises, quizzes, and real-world applications.
- **Offer value-added services** : In addition to the learning plan, provide one-on-one tutoring, career advice, or exam preparation to add value to your services.
- **Market on social media** : Build an online presence by sharing success stories, educational tips, and testimonials from satisfied learners.

By offering personalised learning plans, you can create a high-value, tailored educational experience that addresses each learner's unique needs and goals. Combining AI with interactive content and ongoing support allows you to provide a service that is not only effective but also scalable and profitable.

Chapter 26
Assisting with Research and Data Analysis

Providing research and data analysis services using AI tools like GPT offers significant opportunities to support academics, professionals, and businesses in making informed decisions. With AI's ability to process large amounts of data, generate insights, and summarise information, you can create a profitable business helping clients conduct research, analyse trends, and interpret complex datasets. This summary outlines practical tips, examples, and resources to help you maximise your earning potential in this field.

The Role of AI in Research and Data Analysis

AI tools, such as GPT, can assist in various stages of research and data analysis by:

- **Conducting literature reviews** : AI can summarise academic papers, reports, and articles, providing a comprehensive overview of existing research on a topic.
- **Data extraction and processing** : AI can help sift through vast datasets, identifying key patterns and relevant information for analysis.
- **Trend identification** : AI tools can identify emerging trends and patterns within datasets, providing valuable insights for businesses and researchers.
- **Generating insights** : AI can suggest interpretations of data, offering a starting point for deeper analysis.
- **Writing research summaries** : GPT can quickly generate summaries of research findings, saving time and helping clients focus on decision-making.

Practical Tips to Maximise Earnings from Research and Data Analysis Services

1. **Identify a niche market** : Focus on a specific area such as academic research, market analysis, or financial data analytics. Offering specialised services helps you

attract clients willing to pay for expertise in their sector.

2. **Use AI tools for data cleaning** : AI can automate data cleaning tasks, such as removing duplicates, filling in missing values, or normalising data formats. Offer this as a key part of your service to save clients time.

3. **Offer comprehensive reports** : Provide clients with detailed, AI-generated reports that include data visualisation, trends, and actionable insights. High-quality reporting can help you justify premium pricing.

4. **Stay up-to-date with industry trends** : Use AI to track industry developments and market changes, allowing you to offer clients the latest information and insights.

5. **Provide consultation services** : Along with the research and data analysis, offer consultation services to help clients understand how the insights generated by AI can influence their decisions and strategy.

Example: Market Research for Small Businesses

For small businesses looking to expand into new markets, you can offer a research and data analysis service that includes:

- **Competitor analysis** : Use AI to gather data on competitors, identifying their strengths, weaknesses, and market position.
- **Trend analysis** : Identify current market trends and customer preferences using AI-powered tools to help businesses make data-driven decisions.
- **Customer behaviour insights** : Analyse customer data to provide insights into buying habits, product preferences, and potential areas for business growth.

Resources to Help with Research and Data Analysis

- **Google Scholar** : A resource for accessing academic papers and research articles, ideal for assisting clients with literature reviews.
- **Excel or Google Sheets** : Use these platforms for organising and analysing data.

Combined with AI tools, they offer powerful data analysis capabilities.

- **Kaggle** : A data science community that provides datasets and tools for analysing data, helping you develop skills and resources for complex data analysis.
- **Tableau** : A powerful data visualisation tool that allows you to present data insights in a clear and compelling way, enhancing your reports.
- **GPT-4** : Use GPT-4 to summarise research, extract key insights, and assist with data interpretation. GPT is also useful for generating professional reports and recommendations based on data analysis.

Maximising Earnings from Research and Data Analysis Services

1. **Offer subscription-based services** : Provide clients with regular updates, market reports, or ongoing data analysis. This model generates recurring revenue and keeps clients engaged long-term.
2. **Target businesses and organisations** : Partner with small businesses, startups, or research institutions to provide ongoing data analysis and research support. These

clients often need regular assistance with decision-making and market research.

3. **Develop data visualisation skills** : Learning how to create clear, professional visual representations of data (charts, graphs, etc.) will allow you to offer a more comprehensive service and charge higher fees.

4. **Package your services** : Bundle research and analysis with strategic consulting, marketing recommendations, or business planning services to create high-value offerings.

5. **Focus on delivering actionable insights** : While providing data is important, clients are often more interested in actionable recommendations. Ensure your analysis leads to clear, practical steps they can implement.

Additional Revenue Streams

1. **Academic research support** : Offer services to academics, including literature reviews, data extraction, and research paper summaries. This is particularly useful for students, researchers, and institutions.

183

2. **Data-driven content creation** : Leverage your research to create blog posts, reports, white papers, or case studies for clients, offering them ready-to-publish content.
3. **Financial market analysis** : Provide analysis for investors or businesses looking to understand market trends, stock data, or economic reports.
4. **Social media and web data analysis** : Offer data analysis services for businesses looking to understand their social media engagement, web traffic, or online customer behaviour.
5. **Government or non-profit contracts** : Bid for research and data analysis projects with government agencies or non-profits that need help understanding social issues, demographic changes, or economic impacts.

Leveraging AI for Research and Data Analysis

1. **Automate repetitive tasks** : Use AI to automate data collection, sorting, and preliminary analysis. This allows you to focus on interpreting results and providing higher-level insights to clients.

2. **Summarise large datasets** : AI can quickly process and summarise large amounts of data, making it easier to identify trends and key insights without manually going through every detail.
3. **Generate hypotheses** : GPT can help formulate potential hypotheses based on existing data patterns, providing a starting point for further research.
4. **Predictive analysis** : Offer predictive modelling services by using AI to analyse historical data and forecast future trends, a valuable tool for businesses and researchers.
5. **Create professional reports** : AI can assist in generating professional-grade reports, complete with data visualisation and well-structured summaries, saving you time and improving the quality of your work.

Maximising Success with Research and Data Analysis

- **Offer clear, concise summaries** : Many clients don't have the time to sift through detailed data. Provide clear, actionable summaries that highlight the most important findings.

- **Focus on client-specific solutions** : Tailor your research and analysis to the specific needs and challenges of each client, making your services highly relevant and valuable.
- **Keep up with technology advancements** : Stay informed about the latest AI tools and data analysis software to offer cutting-edge solutions to your clients.
- **Market your services effectively** : Use social media, professional networks, and testimonials to showcase the impact of your research and data analysis services.

Offering AI-powered research and data analysis services can open the door to a wide range of clients, from small businesses to academic institutions. By combining advanced AI tools with your expertise, you can deliver high-quality, actionable insights that help your clients make informed decisions, all while maximising your own earning potential.

Chapter 27
AI-Powered Writing Assistant Tools

AI-powered writing assistant tools have revolutionised the way individuals and businesses approach content creation. These tools use artificial intelligence to assist with everything from grammar and style suggestions to generating complete articles or emails. With their ability to enhance productivity and improve the quality of writing, they offer significant earning potential for freelancers, content creators, and businesses. This summary outlines practical tips, examples, and resources to help you maximise your earning potential by leveraging AI-powered writing assistant tools.

Benefits of AI-Powered Writing Assistant Tools

- **Time efficiency** : AI tools can help writers produce content faster by automating repetitive tasks like proofreading, formatting, and even generating initial drafts.
- **Improved quality** : Writing assistants offer suggestions for grammar, style, tone, and clarity, helping to create polished and professional content.
- **Versatility** : These tools are useful across various writing formats, from blog posts and

social media updates to business reports, emails, and even fiction.

- **Cost-effectiveness** : Using AI can reduce the need for additional editing services, making it a cost-effective solution for businesses and individual writers.

Practical Tips to Maximise Earnings with AI-Powered Writing Tools

1. **Offer content creation services** : Use AI tools to generate articles, blog posts, or website content for clients. By leveraging these tools, you can produce high-quality content quickly and handle a larger workload.
2. **Proofreading and editing** : Use writing assistants like **Grammarly** or **ProWritingAid** to offer proofreading and editing services. These tools can catch errors in grammar, spelling, punctuation, and even suggest style improvements, making your editing services more efficient and thorough.
3. **Expand your service offerings** : Combine AI writing tools with other services like SEO optimisation, email marketing, or content

strategy. AI helps you handle more diverse tasks, increasing your revenue streams.

4. **Specialise in niche industries** : Offer specialised writing services for industries such as tech, healthcare, or finance. AI tools can assist in creating technically accurate content, helping you serve niche markets with more confidence.

5. **Personalise writing tasks** : Use AI assistants to create tailored resumes, cover letters, or business communications for clients, offering a personalised service that is in high demand.

Example: Using AI to Offer Blog Writing Services

AI writing assistants can help you offer blog writing services to clients by:

- **Generating ideas** : AI can assist with brainstorming blog topics based on trending keywords or client input.
- **Creating drafts** : Tools like **Jasper AI** can generate drafts of blog posts based on specific topics, saving you time while ensuring high-quality output.
- **Improving SEO** : AI writing tools can offer suggestions for optimising content with

keywords, metadata, and readability improvements, making your posts more discoverable online.

Resources to Help with AI-Powered Writing Assistant Tools

- **Grammarly** : An AI-powered tool that checks grammar, punctuation, and style, providing real-time suggestions to improve writing clarity and tone.
- **ProWritingAid** : Offers a detailed analysis of your writing, including grammar, readability, and style suggestions, making it ideal for longer content such as essays or reports.
- **Jasper AI (formerly Jarvis)** : A content creation tool that helps generate blog posts, marketing copy, and product descriptions. It's excellent for speeding up the writing process.
- **Writesonic** : An AI tool designed to create marketing copy, social media posts, and blog articles. It's suitable for freelancers looking to deliver large volumes of content.
- **Hemingway App** : A tool that focuses on improving readability by highlighting complex sentences and passive voice,

making your writing more concise and engaging.

Maximising Earnings with AI-Powered Writing Assistant Tools

1. **Increase your workload** : By using AI to speed up writing tasks, you can take on more clients or projects, increasing your overall output and earnings.
2. **Offer premium services** : Provide clients with AI-assisted content creation services, such as creating high-quality articles, web copy, or social media posts quickly and efficiently, and charge premium prices for faster delivery.
3. **Develop a subscription model** : Offer clients ongoing writing services on a subscription basis, using AI tools to regularly update their blog or website with fresh content. This can generate steady, recurring income.
4. **Use AI for multilingual content** : Many AI writing assistants offer translation capabilities. This allows you to offer services in multiple languages, expanding your client base internationally.

5. **Sell AI-generated templates** : Create and sell templates for emails, social media posts, resumes, or other business communications. AI can help you create a range of templates tailored to different industries or needs, which can be sold as digital products.

Additional Revenue Streams

1. **Ghostwriting services** : Use AI tools to ghostwrite books, articles, or content for clients who need polished writing without the time to create it themselves.
2. **Business communications** : Provide AI-assisted services for drafting professional emails, internal reports, and business proposals, targeting entrepreneurs and small businesses.
3. **Content repurposing** : Use AI to help repurpose content for different platforms. For instance, transform a blog post into a series of social media updates or a newsletter, maximising the value of each piece of content.
4. **Online courses and tutorials** : Create educational content, such as online courses

or how-to guides, that teaches others how to effectively use AI-powered writing tools for their own businesses or projects.

5. **Affiliate marketing** : If you use and promote AI writing tools like Grammarly or Jasper AI, you can earn commissions by recommending these tools to others through affiliate marketing programmes.

Leveraging AI for AI-Powered Writing Assistant Tools

1. **Automate repetitive tasks** : Use AI to automate tasks like proofreading, grammar checks, or even content generation for repetitive writing jobs, such as product descriptions or email templates.

2. **Scale your business** : With AI, you can increase your output without significantly increasing your workload, allowing you to scale your business and take on more clients.

3. **Customise tone and style** : AI tools can help tailor content to specific tones, such as professional, conversational, or creative, allowing you to meet the unique demands of different clients.

4. **Generate outlines** : Use AI to create content outlines for longer projects, such as

eBooks, white papers, or academic papers, ensuring the structure is sound before writing begins.
5. **AI-assisted collaboration** : If working with teams, AI tools can streamline collaboration by ensuring consistent tone, style, and quality across all contributors.

Maximising Success with AI-Powered Writing Assistant Tools

- **Offer fast turnaround** : One of the main benefits of AI is speed. Advertise fast turnaround times to attract clients who need content quickly.
- **Focus on quality** : While AI can assist with content generation, always review and refine the output to ensure it meets your client's standards and expectations.
- **Upskill continuously** : Stay updated with the latest AI tools and features. The better you understand how to use these tools, the more efficiently you can produce high-quality content.
- **Market your services online** : Build a professional website or social media presence that showcases your ability to use

AI tools to create high-quality, efficient writing services.

By using AI-powered writing assistant tools effectively, you can dramatically increase your productivity, reduce the time spent on writing and editing, and offer high-value services to a broader client base. This combination of efficiency, quality, and scalability can help you maximise your earning potential in the growing field of AI-assisted content creation.

Chapter 28
Customised Social Media Captions

Creating customised social media captions is an essential service in today's digital marketing landscape. Social media platforms rely heavily on engaging, well-crafted captions to capture attention, encourage interaction, and drive engagement. By offering custom caption-writing services tailored to specific audiences and brands, you can help businesses stand out and connect with their audience. This summary provides practical tips, examples, and resources to help you maximise your earning potential by providing customised social media captions.

Importance of Customised Social Media Captions

- **Increased engagement** : Well-crafted captions can significantly boost likes, shares, comments, and overall interaction with a post.
- **Brand voice consistency** : Custom captions help maintain a consistent brand voice across different platforms, reinforcing brand identity and messaging.
- **Optimisation for algorithms** : Customised captions can be optimised for platform algorithms by incorporating trending hashtags, keywords, and calls to action, improving reach and visibility.
- **Directing traffic** : Captions can guide users towards specific actions, such as visiting a website, signing up for a newsletter, or purchasing a product, driving conversions.

Practical Tips to Maximise Earnings from Custom Social Media Captions

1. **Understand the brand voice** : Tailor each caption to reflect the unique tone and voice of the brand, whether it's formal, casual, or

playful. This personalisation is key to creating meaningful engagement.

2. **Leverage platform-specific strategies** : Each social media platform has its unique style. Instagram may benefit from visually-driven, short captions, whereas LinkedIn requires a more professional tone. Offer captions optimised for each platform.

3. **Incorporate trending topics and hashtags** : Keep up with trending hashtags and relevant topics within the brand's industry. Use these elements to increase post visibility and relevance, ensuring your captions reach a wider audience.

4. **Focus on engagement-driven language** : Craft captions that encourage users to like, share, comment, or engage with a call to action (CTA). Ask questions, use polls, or invite users to tag a friend, all of which increase interaction.

5. **Offer a content calendar service** : Expand your offerings by providing a full social media content calendar that includes not only captions but also recommended posting schedules and hashtags. This can become a high-value service for businesses looking for an organised approach to social media.

Example: Writing Captions for an Instagram Brand

For a fashion brand on Instagram, you could write captions like:

- **Short and snappy** : "Ready to rock the latest trends? □ Check out our new collection! #FashionGoals #NewArrivals"
- **Engagement-focused** : "Which look is your favourite? Comment below and let us know! □ #OOTD #FashionInspo"
- **Brand promotion** : "Discover timeless pieces made just for you. Shop the collection now! □□ #ShopNow #SustainableFashion"

These captions combine a strong call to action, brand voice consistency, and hashtag strategy to maximise engagement and reach.

Resources to Help with Customised Social Media Captions

- **Later** : A social media scheduling tool that can help you plan and publish captions across multiple platforms, allowing for better organisation and execution.

- **Hashtagify** : Use this tool to find trending and relevant hashtags to include in your captions, improving post visibility.
- **Canva** : While primarily a design tool, Canva offers social media templates that help you pair visuals with engaging captions, streamlining content creation.
- **BuzzSumo** : A content research tool that helps identify trending topics and viral content in specific niches, providing inspiration for timely and relevant captions.
- **Social Blade** : Provides insights into social media metrics, helping you track the success of your captions in terms of engagement and reach.

Maximising Earnings from Custom Social Media Caption Services

1. **Create packages** : Offer different pricing tiers based on the number of captions, platforms, or engagement strategies included. You can offer monthly packages that include regular updates and captions across multiple platforms.

2. **Niche expertise** : Specialise in a particular industry, such as beauty, fitness, or tech, where you can develop expertise in the voice and trends that resonate with that market, allowing you to charge a premium for your knowledge.
3. **Collaborate with influencers** : Work with influencers who need personalised captions for their social media posts. They often require a professional touch to align with their personal brand and audience.
4. **Offer real-time support** : Provide clients with on-demand caption writing services for real-time events or campaigns, such as product launches or sales. This allows you to charge for timely, high-priority services.
5. **Run social media audits** : Offer a service that reviews a brand's current social media presence, identifying where caption improvements can be made. This can lead to ongoing caption-writing work as you help businesses optimise their social content.

Additional Revenue Streams

1. **Content strategy consultation** : Use your experience in writing captions to offer full

social media content strategies, advising clients on how to structure their posts, when to post, and how to engage with their audience effectively.

2. **Copywriting for ads** : Expand into writing short-form copy for social media advertisements, such as Facebook or Instagram ads, where concise, persuasive writing is key to driving conversions.

3. **Social media management** : Offer full social media management services, where you not only write captions but also handle content scheduling, community management, and performance analysis.

4. **Workshops or courses** : Create workshops or online courses teaching small businesses how to craft effective social media captions, leveraging your expertise to reach a broader audience.

5. **Affiliate marketing** : Partner with social media tools or platforms to recommend them to your clients, earning commissions through affiliate programmes.

Leveraging AI for Custom Social Media Captions

1. **AI-powered caption generation** : Use AI tools such as **Jasper AI** or **Copy.ai** to

generate initial ideas for captions, which can then be personalised and refined to suit the client's brand and goals.

2. **A/B testing captions** : Experiment with different versions of captions using AI-driven tools that analyse which phrases or calls to action result in higher engagement, allowing you to refine your approach.

3. **Optimising for tone and length** : AI tools like **Grammarly** or **Hemingway** can ensure that your captions are concise, engaging, and suited to the platform's tone.

4. **Personalisation at scale** : For clients who need a large volume of captions, AI tools can help you create content faster, allowing you to take on more work without compromising on quality.

5. **Sentiment analysis** : AI tools can help analyse audience sentiment in response to certain types of posts, enabling you to write captions that resonate emotionally with your target audience.

Maximising Success with Custom Social Media Captions

- **Track performance metrics** : Regularly review how your captions perform in terms of engagement, reach, and conversions. Use these insights to adjust and improve your strategies for future posts.

- **Stay on top of trends** : Follow industry influencers, hashtags, and social media trends to ensure your captions are timely and relevant.
- **Tailor to audience needs** : Customise captions to reflect the specific interests and behaviours of the audience on each platform. For example, Instagram users might respond to casual and visual captions, while LinkedIn users might prefer a more formal and informative tone.
- **Build a portfolio** : Showcase your caption-writing success with case studies or testimonials from clients who saw improved engagement and growth due to your work.

By offering customised social media captions, you can help brands elevate their online presence, engage with their audience more effectively, and drive better results from their social media campaigns. When combined with strategic marketing and AI-powered tools, this service can become a highly lucrative addition to your freelance or business portfolio.

Chapter 29
Writing Reviews and Testimonials

Writing reviews and testimonials is a valuable service for businesses looking to build credibility, trust, and social proof. Reviews help potential customers make informed decisions, while testimonials provide authentic, positive experiences that can sway their choices. As a service provider, you can offer well-crafted reviews and testimonials to enhance a brand's online reputation, boost conversion rates, and influence buyer decisions. This summary includes practical tips, examples, and resources to help you maximise your earning potential by writing reviews and testimonials.

Importance of Reviews and Testimonials

- **Builds trust** : Honest, well-written reviews and testimonials provide potential customers with the confidence to make purchasing decisions, knowing that others have had positive experiences.
- **Boosts credibility** : Testimonials from satisfied clients enhance a business's reputation, giving them an edge in competitive markets.
- **Improves SEO** : User-generated content, such as reviews, can improve a website's

ranking on search engines, increasing visibility and driving traffic.

- **Encourages conversions** : Reviews and testimonials can directly influence purchasing behaviour by highlighting the benefits of a product or service, leading to higher conversion rates.

Practical Tips to Maximise Earnings from Writing Reviews and Testimonials

1. **Understand the audience** : Tailor reviews and testimonials to the specific audience or market. For example, a tech-savvy audience might prefer more detailed, feature-oriented reviews, while lifestyle audiences may appreciate a focus on user experience.
2. **Highlight benefits** : Focus on how the product or service solved a problem or met a need. Effective testimonials highlight the key benefits that resonate with potential customers.
3. **Incorporate storytelling** : Testimonials are more impactful when they include personal stories or specific examples of how a product or service has positively impacted the user.

4. **Keep it authentic** : Authenticity is crucial in reviews and testimonials. Use natural language and avoid over-embellishment to maintain trustworthiness.
5. **Optimise for platforms** : Reviews written for different platforms, such as Google, Yelp, or Amazon, should meet the specific requirements of those platforms. For instance, Amazon reviews need to be product-focused, while Yelp reviews may benefit from highlighting the customer service experience.
6. **Include data** : Where applicable, include quantifiable results in testimonials, such as "Since using this software, my productivity has increased by 50%." This adds credibility and makes the testimonial more persuasive.

Example: Writing Reviews and Testimonials for an E-commerce Store

For an online store selling fitness equipment, you might write a review like:

- **Review** : "I've been using this treadmill for 3 months, and it's exceeded my expectations. The build quality is excellent, and the range of preset workouts has kept me motivated. The incline feature is a great bonus for high-intensity sessions. Highly recommend!"

- **Testimonial** : "As a personal trainer, I needed reliable equipment for my home gym, and this treadmill has been a game-changer. It's sturdy, easy to use, and offers all the features I need for my clients and myself. The customer service was also outstanding. Definitely worth the investment!"

Both examples highlight product benefits, include personal experiences, and maintain authenticity, making them effective for influencing other buyers.

Resources to Help with Writing Reviews and Testimonials

- **Trustpilot** : A platform where users can write and read reviews. It offers guidelines on crafting reviews that meet their authenticity standards.
- **Google Reviews** : Google My Business allows businesses to collect customer reviews, and they provide tips on writing impactful feedback for SEO purposes.

- **Yelp** : Specialises in local business reviews, and it offers a set of guidelines for creating detailed and useful reviews.
- **Amazon** : As one of the largest e-commerce platforms, Amazon provides a structured format for writing product reviews, which often include ratings, pros, and cons.

Maximising Earnings from Writing Reviews and Testimonials

1. **Offer review-writing packages** : Create tiered packages based on the number of reviews or platforms covered. For example, you could offer reviews for Google, Amazon, and Facebook as a bundle.
2. **Work with businesses** : Partner with small and medium-sized businesses to help them build a collection of authentic testimonials from their customers. Many companies are willing to pay for expertly crafted testimonials that enhance their credibility.
3. **Specialise in niche markets** : Focus on industries such as tech, beauty, or travel, where reviews and testimonials play a crucial role in consumer decisions.

Specialising allows you to charge premium rates for your expertise.

4. **Provide ghostwriting services** : Offer ghostwriting for clients who want to share their positive experiences but need help articulating their thoughts. This is especially valuable for high-profile clients or businesses.

5. **Affiliate reviews** : Write product reviews for affiliate marketing programmes. You can create blog posts or social media content reviewing products, earning commissions on referred sales.

Additional Revenue Streams

1. **Review blog** : Create a niche blog focused on product reviews, offering in-depth insights and comparisons. Monetise the blog through affiliate links, sponsored content, or ads.

2. **Video testimonials** : Offer clients video testimonial scripts, helping them produce compelling video content that features customer experiences.

3. **Product comparison content** : Write comparison reviews that evaluate similar products, guiding potential customers

towards making purchasing decisions. This is popular in industries like technology and home appliances.

4. **Course creation** : Develop a course or workshop teaching small businesses how to gather and use customer testimonials effectively in their marketing materials.

5. **Social proof strategies** : Consult businesses on how to use social proof, including reviews and testimonials, across their websites, ads, and emails to build trust with their audience.

Leveraging AI for Writing Reviews and Testimonials

1. **AI-generated drafts** : Use AI tools such as **Jasper AI** or **Writesonic** to generate initial drafts of reviews and testimonials, which can be refined and personalised for specific products or services.

2. **Sentiment analysis** : AI tools can analyse customer feedback from surveys or social media to identify common positive themes, helping you craft more genuine and targeted reviews.

3. **Time efficiency** : AI tools allow you to create reviews and testimonials quickly,

enabling you to take on more projects without sacrificing quality.

4. **Customisation at scale** : For clients with a high volume of products, AI can assist in creating consistent yet customised reviews for each item, maintaining authenticity while speeding up the process.

5. **Multilingual reviews** : Offer reviews and testimonials in multiple languages using AI translation tools, expanding your client base to international businesses.

Maximising Success with Writing Reviews and Testimonials

- **Stay updated on review guidelines** : Different platforms, such as Google, Yelp, and Amazon, have specific rules about review writing. Ensure you stay compliant with their guidelines to avoid removal or rejection of reviews.
- **Balance detail and brevity** : Reviews should be detailed enough to be informative but concise enough to keep readers' attention. Use bullet points or short paragraphs to enhance readability.
- **Build trust with authenticity** : Always focus on delivering authentic reviews. If you're

ghostwriting testimonials, ensure the client's voice and experience are reflected accurately.

- **Track review impact** : Encourage clients to track how reviews and testimonials influence their sales, conversions, or website traffic. This data can be used to refine your review-writing strategies and showcase your value to future clients.

By offering professional review and testimonial writing services, you can help businesses build trust and influence buyer decisions. Combining your writing expertise with strategic marketing and AI tools, you can expand your offerings and increase your earning potential in this high-demand field.

Chapter 30
Creating AI-Driven Product Suggestions

AI-driven product suggestions are a powerful tool used by e-commerce platforms to enhance the customer experience and increase sales. By leveraging AI algorithms, businesses can offer personalised product recommendations based on customer preferences, browsing history, and purchasing behaviour. Offering AI-powered product suggestion services can help businesses optimise their sales strategies, improve customer satisfaction, and increase conversion rates. This summary provides practical tips, examples, and resources to help you maximise your earning potential in this field.

Importance of AI-Driven Product Suggestions

- **Personalised shopping experiences** : AI algorithms can analyse customer data to make product recommendations that are tailored to individual preferences, leading to a more personalised and satisfying shopping experience.
- **Increased sales and conversions** : Personalised product suggestions have been shown to boost average order values and conversion rates by offering customers products they are more likely to purchase.
- **Improved customer retention** : Customers are more likely to return to a website that consistently recommends relevant products, improving customer loyalty and retention.
- **Efficient cross-selling and upselling** : AI can identify complementary products or upgrades, encouraging customers to

purchase additional items or more
expensive options.

Practical Tips to Maximise Earnings from AI-Driven Product Suggestions

1. **Understand customer behaviour** : The success of product recommendations relies on a deep understanding of customer behaviour, including their browsing patterns, previous purchases, and preferences. Ensure that your AI models are trained on diverse data sources to deliver accurate suggestions.
2. **Leverage multiple recommendation strategies** : Implement various AI recommendation strategies, such as collaborative filtering (based on customer similarities), content-based filtering (based on product attributes), and hybrid models that combine both approaches. This variety ensures a well-rounded recommendation system.
3. **Segment customers** : Divide customers into segments based on their preferences, demographics, or purchase history. Offer AI-driven recommendations for each segment

to increase the relevance and appeal of the suggestions.

4. **Optimise for mobile platforms** : Many customers shop on mobile devices, so ensure your AI-driven recommendation system is optimised for mobile platforms to create seamless shopping experiences across all devices.

5. **A/B testing for recommendations** : Continuously test different product recommendation strategies and placements (e.g., homepage, cart, or product page) to identify the most effective configurations. Data from these tests can help you refine and improve your AI-driven suggestions.

Example: AI-Driven Product Suggestions in E-commerce

For an online clothing retailer, an AI system could suggest:

- **Related items** : If a customer is viewing a specific dress, the AI might recommend shoes, accessories, or jackets that complement it.
- **Similar products** : Based on a customer's browsing history, the AI can suggest similar

items in different colours, styles, or price ranges.

- **Upselling options** : When a customer is viewing a product, the AI might suggest a higher-end version or an upgraded model with additional features.
- **Frequently bought together** : AI can recommend items that are often purchased together, such as a complete outfit (shirt, trousers, and shoes) when a customer adds a single item to their cart.

Resources to Help with AI-Driven Product Suggestions

- **Google Cloud AI** : Provides tools for building and integrating machine learning models that can be used for product recommendations.
- **AWS Personalize** : Amazon Web Services offers a machine learning service that allows developers to create custom product recommendation systems.
- **Algolia Recommend** : This API helps businesses deliver personalised product suggestions by using search and recommendation data.

- **Shopify App Store** : Offers AI-powered recommendation tools such as "Frequently Bought Together" and "Product Upsell" that can be easily integrated into Shopify stores.
- **Python and TensorFlow** : Use Python with machine learning frameworks like TensorFlow to develop your own AI-driven product recommendation systems.

Maximising Earnings from AI-Driven Product Suggestion Services

1. **Offer integration services** : Businesses may need help integrating AI product suggestion tools into their existing websites or platforms. Providing setup and integration services can be a high-demand offering.
2. **Custom AI model development** : Offer to build customised AI recommendation models tailored to specific business needs or customer behaviours. This adds value for companies looking for unique solutions rather than off-the-shelf tools.
3. **Data analysis and strategy consulting** : Provide data analysis and consulting services to help businesses optimise their use of AI-driven recommendations. You can

offer insights on how customer data can be leveraged to refine and improve recommendations.

4. **Subscription-based services** : Offer ongoing support and optimisation for AI recommendation systems, such as continuous A/B testing, model tuning, and performance tracking, on a subscription basis.

5. **Work with niche industries** : Certain industries, such as fashion, electronics, or beauty, can benefit significantly from highly personalised recommendations. Specialising in these niches allows you to charge premium rates for your expertise.

Additional Revenue Streams

1. **E-commerce optimisation** : Alongside AI-driven product suggestions, offer broader e-commerce optimisation services, such as improving website navigation, user experience, or conversion rates.

2. **Affiliate marketing recommendations** : Provide AI-powered product recommendations for affiliate marketing websites, helping increase sales

commissions by improving the relevance of suggested products.

3. **AI consulting** : Offer consulting services for businesses looking to incorporate AI into their sales and marketing strategies, beyond just product recommendations.

4. **Recommendation as a service** : Create a product recommendation engine that can be licensed to multiple businesses on a SaaS (Software as a Service) basis.

5. **Educational courses** : Develop online courses teaching businesses how to implement and optimise AI-driven product suggestions in their e-commerce operations.

Leveraging AI for Product Suggestions

1. **Use machine learning libraries** : Tools like **scikit-learn** and **TensorFlow** allow developers to create machine learning models that power recommendation systems.

2. **Automate data collection** : AI systems can automatically collect and analyse customer data from multiple sources, including web browsing history, social media interactions, and past purchases, to refine product recommendations.

3. **Personalisation at scale** : AI allows for product suggestions to be personalised for thousands or even millions of customers simultaneously, providing individualised experiences without manual intervention.
4. **Predict future needs** : AI can use predictive analytics to suggest products that customers might need in the future, based on their previous behaviour and broader consumer trends.
5. **Real-time recommendations** : AI systems can provide real-time product recommendations based on current browsing sessions or interactions, increasing the chances of a purchase during that session.

Maximising Success with AI-Driven Product Suggestions

- **Monitor recommendation performance** : Regularly review key metrics such as click-through rates, conversion rates, and average order values to measure the effectiveness of AI-driven suggestions.
- **Refine models regularly** : Continuously train and refine your AI models using the

latest customer data to ensure recommendations remain accurate and relevant.

- **Prioritise user experience** : Ensure that AI-driven product suggestions are presented in a way that enhances the customer's experience without being intrusive or overwhelming.
- **Adapt to seasonality** : Adjust product recommendation algorithms to reflect seasonal trends, holidays, or special promotions. AI systems can automatically detect and respond to these changes in customer behaviour.
- **Build trust through transparency** : Be transparent with customers about how their data is used to generate product recommendations. This builds trust and encourages more engagement with your suggestions.

By offering AI-driven product suggestion services, you can help businesses improve customer satisfaction, boost sales, and increase loyalty. Combining your expertise with AI tools and strategic marketing insights, you can build a highly profitable and scalable business in this growing field.

Chapter 31

Providing AI Content Consulting

AI content consulting is a rapidly growing field where consultants help businesses harness the power of artificial intelligence to enhance their content creation, optimisation, and distribution processes. As more businesses realise the potential of AI to improve efficiency, personalise experiences, and scale content production, there is a high demand for experts who can guide them in implementing AI-powered solutions. This summary offers practical tips, examples, and resources to help you maximise your earning potential as an AI content consultant.

Importance of AI Content Consulting

- **Increased efficiency** : AI-driven tools can automate time-consuming content tasks such as idea generation, writing, editing, and SEO optimisation, freeing up human resources for more strategic activities.
- **Personalised content** : AI allows businesses to create highly personalised content for their target audience by analysing user data, preferences, and behaviour.

- **Scalability** : AI can help companies produce large amounts of content across multiple platforms, enabling them to scale without increasing their workforce significantly.
- **Improved content strategy** : AI analytics provide deep insights into content performance, helping businesses refine their strategies based on data-driven decisions.

Practical Tips to Maximise Earnings from AI Content Consulting

1. **Specialise in AI tools** : Become proficient in popular AI-powered content tools such as **Jasper AI** , **Writesonic** , **Copy.ai** , and **Surfer SEO** . Offering expertise in these tools allows you to provide tailored recommendations to businesses seeking to streamline content creation.
2. **Offer full-service packages** : Provide comprehensive consulting services that cover the entire content lifecycle—from content ideation and creation to optimisation, distribution, and performance tracking. Businesses are more likely to invest in full packages that cover all aspects of content management.

3. **Tailor your services to different industries** : Each industry has unique content needs. Tailor your AI content consulting services to specific niches, such as e-commerce, finance, healthcare, or real estate. Specialisation can help you stand out and command higher fees.

4. **Provide training and support** : Offer training sessions or workshops for in-house teams on how to use AI-powered content tools effectively. Many businesses want to adopt AI but need assistance with implementation and best practices.

5. **Leverage analytics** : Use AI-powered analytics tools like **Google Analytics** , **HubSpot** , and **Clearscope** to help clients monitor their content's performance. This data can be used to refine strategies, making your consultancy more valuable by offering measurable results.

6. **Stay updated with AI advancements** : The AI landscape evolves quickly, so staying current with the latest AI tools, trends, and developments will help you offer cutting-edge advice and maintain your competitive edge.

Example: AI Content Consulting for a Blog

For a business looking to scale its content marketing through blogging, an AI content consultant could:

- **Content ideation** : Use AI-powered tools like **BuzzSumo** or **Frase** to identify trending topics and keywords that align with the business's goals.
- **Content creation** : Recommend tools like **Jasper AI** to help generate initial drafts or SEO-optimised blog posts, which can be refined by human editors.
- **Optimisation** : Integrate **Surfer SEO** to optimise blog posts for search engines, ensuring higher rankings and increased organic traffic.
- **Performance tracking** : Use **Google Analytics** to monitor blog traffic, reader engagement, and conversion rates, helping the client refine their content strategy.

Resources to Help with AI Content Consulting

- **Jasper AI** : A leading AI-powered writing tool that helps create blog posts, product descriptions, emails, and more.
- **Surfer SEO** : An AI-based tool that optimises content for search engines by analysing top-performing pages and suggesting improvements.
- **Copy.ai** : An AI copywriting tool that can assist with writing ad copy, social media posts, and longer-form content like articles and blogs.
- **BuzzSumo** : A content research tool that identifies popular topics, influencers, and competitors' top-performing content.
- **Frase** : An AI tool that helps with content research and creation, optimising articles for SEO and improving their readability.

Maximising Earnings from AI Content Consulting

1. **Consulting retainers** : Offer monthly retainer packages where businesses pay for ongoing AI content consulting services. This can include regular content audits, strategy

updates, and performance reviews, providing a steady income stream.

2. **Content strategy development** : Help clients develop long-term content strategies using AI analytics and prediction models to identify content opportunities, target audiences, and distribution channels.

3. **Offer AI integration services** : Assist businesses in integrating AI tools into their existing content management systems (CMS). This could include configuring automation tools and training staff to use them effectively.

4. **Partner with agencies** : Collaborate with digital marketing agencies to offer AI content consulting as an additional service. This expands your client base and offers opportunities for ongoing projects.

5. **Develop AI content products** : Create your own content templates or AI-generated content resources, such as guides or e-books, that businesses can purchase to streamline their content processes.

Additional Revenue Streams

1. **Content optimisation services** : Offer AI-powered content optimisation services to

businesses looking to improve their existing content. This could involve reworking blog posts, product descriptions, or social media posts using AI tools to improve readability, SEO, and engagement.

2. **Custom AI tools** : Work with developers to build custom AI content tools that cater to specific industries or client needs. This could include niche content generators or industry-specific SEO tools.

3. **Online courses** : Develop courses that teach businesses how to integrate AI into their content strategies. These can be monetised through platforms like Udemy or by offering exclusive training to clients.

4. **Affiliate marketing** : Promote AI content tools through affiliate links on your website, blog, or social media. Earn commissions by recommending tools like Jasper AI or Surfer SEO.

5. **AI content auditing** : Offer content audits that leverage AI analytics to identify gaps, opportunities, and optimisation areas. Clients can use these audits to refine their content strategies.

Leveraging AI for Content Consulting

1. **AI-powered content automation** : Use AI to automate content tasks like topic research, drafting, and keyword optimisation. This allows clients to produce high-quality content faster and with less effort.
2. **Data-driven content** : AI tools can analyse massive amounts of data to identify what content performs well. Use this data to advise clients on what topics, formats, or keywords will likely generate the best results.
3. **Personalisation at scale** : Help businesses create personalised content for different audience segments by using AI to analyse user data and behaviour. This enhances the relevance and engagement of the content.
4. **Content repurposing** : Use AI tools to repurpose existing content across different formats. For example, AI can help turn a blog post into a social media post, infographic, or video script, maximising the value of the content.
5. **AI-assisted content editing** : Tools like **Grammarly** or **ProWritingAid** use AI to help refine and polish content, ensuring it

meets high standards of grammar, tone, and readability.

Maximising Success with AI Content Consulting

- **Measure and report ROI** : Businesses want to see tangible results from their investment in AI content consulting. Use analytics tools to track the impact of your recommendations, such as improved traffic, higher conversions, or increased engagement.
- **Customise solutions** : Tailor AI content strategies to each client's specific needs, industry, and goals. A one-size-fits-all approach won't work, so focus on creating personalised strategies that deliver measurable results.
- **Stay ethical with AI use** : While AI tools can produce content quickly, always emphasise the importance of maintaining quality and authenticity. Ensure that the content remains engaging and valuable to the audience.
- **Emphasise human oversight** : AI is a powerful tool, but human oversight is essential to ensure content aligns with brand voice, values, and goals. Position yourself

as the expert who can help businesses strike the right balance between AI automation and human creativity.

By providing AI content consulting services, you can help businesses transform their content strategies, enhance efficiency, and personalise their outreach. With expertise in AI tools, industry trends, and strategic consulting, you can build a profitable and in-demand service offering in this exciting and evolving field.

Chapter 32
Creating AI-Powered Websites or Blogs

AI-powered websites and blogs represent the future of online content, allowing businesses and individuals to create, manage, and optimise their web presence with increased efficiency. Leveraging AI in website and blog development can streamline content generation, improve SEO performance, enhance user experience, and offer personalised content to visitors. This summary provides practical tips, examples, and resources to help you maximise your earning potential by creating AI-powered websites or blogs.

Importance of AI-Powered Websites and Blogs

- **Automated content creation** : AI tools can generate high-quality, SEO-optimised content quickly, reducing the need for constant manual updates.
- **Improved SEO** : AI-powered platforms can analyse search trends and optimise content for better visibility on search engines.
- **Personalised user experiences** : AI can personalise content recommendations and tailor the site's user experience based on individual browsing behaviours and preferences.
- **Enhanced site performance** : AI tools can monitor site performance in real time, providing suggestions to improve loading times, design, and overall functionality.
- **Efficient content management** : AI can automate tasks such as scheduling posts, managing comments, and handling customer queries via chatbots.

Practical Tips to Maximise Earnings from AI-Powered Websites and Blogs

1. **Offer end-to-end services** : Provide complete services, including the setup, customisation, and maintenance of AI-powered websites or blogs. Clients often prefer working with a single provider for all aspects of website development.
2. **Focus on niche markets** : Tailor your AI-powered websites or blogs to specific industries such as e-commerce, finance, health, or travel. By specialising in a niche, you can offer unique solutions that address the specific needs of that industry.
3. **Use AI to boost engagement** : Implement AI-powered chatbots, content recommendation systems, and personalised newsletters to engage visitors and increase conversion rates.
4. **Utilise AI-driven SEO** : Tools like **Surfer SEO** , **MarketMuse** , and **Clearscope** use AI to optimise websites and blogs for search engines, ensuring that your clients' sites rank higher in search results.
5. **Monetise AI-driven blogs** : Help clients generate revenue through affiliate marketing, ads, or sponsored content by

utilising AI tools to optimise and increase traffic to their blogs.

6. **Automate routine tasks** : Offer AI-driven solutions to automate content updates, social media postings, and other routine tasks to save time and increase efficiency.

Example: AI-Powered Website Creation

For a business looking to create an e-commerce site:

- **Content automation** : Use AI tools like **Jasper AI** or **Writesonic** to create product descriptions, blog posts, and category pages.
- **Personalisation** : Implement AI systems that recommend products or content based on individual visitor preferences and browsing history.
- **SEO optimisation** : Use AI-powered SEO tools like **Surfer SEO** to ensure that product descriptions and blog content are optimised for search engines.
- **Customer support** : Deploy AI chatbots such as **Tidio** or **Drift** to assist customers with queries, improving customer

satisfaction and freeing up human resources for more complex tasks.

Resources to Help with AI-Powered Websites and Blogs

- **Jasper AI** : A content generation tool that can write blogs, landing pages, product descriptions, and more, with SEO in mind.
- **WordPress Plugins** : Use AI-powered WordPress plugins such as **RankMath** for SEO, **WP-Chatbot** for customer interactions, and **Jetpack** for analytics.
- **Surfer SEO** : A tool that helps optimise content with AI-based recommendations to improve rankings.
- **Writesonic** : AI writing software that automates content creation for blogs, product descriptions, and more.
- **Tidio** : An AI-powered chatbot solution that can be integrated into websites to handle customer inquiries and boost engagement.

Maximising Earnings from AI-Powered Website and Blog Creation

1. **Subscription-based maintenance services** : Offer ongoing support and maintenance for AI-powered websites, including content updates, SEO optimisation, and performance tracking. This provides a steady income stream while keeping clients' websites up-to-date.
2. **Custom AI solutions** : Develop bespoke AI tools or features that cater to specific client needs, such as custom recommendation engines, smart search features, or automated content curation systems.
3. **Offer training packages** : Provide training on how to use AI tools effectively, teaching clients how to manage their AI-powered blogs and websites independently or alongside your services.
4. **Create niche AI-driven blog platforms** : Develop and sell pre-built AI-powered blog templates for specific industries, such as personal blogs, travel blogs, or business websites.
5. **Upsell additional AI features** : Offer premium services such as advanced personalisation tools, AI-driven analytics dashboards, or integrations with CRM

systems, charging higher rates for more sophisticated solutions.

Additional Revenue Streams

1. **Affiliate marketing** : Monetise your AI-powered blogs by recommending relevant products or services, earning commissions through affiliate links. AI tools can help identify the most suitable products to recommend.
2. **Ad management** : Use AI tools to optimise ad placements on websites or blogs. Tools like **Google AdSense** can be automated to generate revenue efficiently through targeted ads.
3. **Online courses** : Create and sell courses that teach individuals or businesses how to build and optimise AI-powered websites and blogs, leveraging platforms like Udemy or Skillshare.
4. **AI consulting** : Offer AI content and website consulting services to businesses looking to incorporate AI into their digital marketing strategies.
5. **Content syndication** : Help clients repurpose and distribute AI-generated

content across multiple platforms, driving more traffic and increasing visibility.

Leveraging AI for Website and Blog Development

1. **AI-powered design tools** : Tools like **Wix ADI** or **Bookmark AiDA** use AI to create custom website designs tailored to a client's brand. This speeds up the design process and ensures a polished final product.
2. **Predictive analytics** : AI tools can predict user behaviour and recommend content or products that align with their interests. Implementing this feature can help websites convert visitors into customers.
3. **Automated SEO** : AI can automatically optimise on-page elements such as keywords, meta tags, and image alt text. This saves time and helps ensure the website ranks well in search engines.
4. **Personalisation engines** : Implement AI engines that customise the user experience based on past behaviour, ensuring visitors receive relevant content and product suggestions.
5. **Content scheduling** : Use AI to schedule and publish blog posts or other updates

automatically, ensuring a consistent content flow without manual intervention.

Maximising Success with AI-Powered Websites and Blogs

- **Monitor and refine AI systems** : Continuously monitor the performance of AI-powered features, using analytics tools to track engagement, traffic, and conversions. Adjust AI models based on this data for better results.
- **Focus on user experience** : AI can greatly improve user experience, but it's essential to balance automation with human oversight to ensure the content remains valuable and authentic.
- **Keep AI systems updated** : As AI technology evolves, ensure the tools and systems you use are up-to-date and compatible with the latest industry standards.
- **Be transparent with AI usage** : Clearly communicate with clients and users how AI is being used on their websites or blogs. Transparency helps build trust and confidence in the AI features you implement.

By offering AI-powered website and blog creation services, you can help businesses save time, improve efficiency, and boost user engagement. With a comprehensive understanding of AI tools, a strategic approach, and a focus on high-quality content, you can build a profitable and future-proof service offering in this exciting space.

Chapter 33
Automating Business Workflows with GPT

Leveraging GPT (Generative Pretrained Transformer) technology to automate business workflows is a powerful way to increase efficiency, reduce costs, and streamline processes. From customer support to data analysis, GPT can be integrated into various business operations to automate routine tasks, allowing human resources to focus on more strategic activities. This summary provides practical tips, examples, and resources to help you maximise your earning potential through the automation of business workflows with GPT.

Importance of Automating Business Workflows with GPT

- **Time-saving automation** : GPT models can handle repetitive tasks such as generating reports, drafting emails, or managing customer queries, reducing the need for manual intervention.
- **Enhanced accuracy** : AI-driven automation reduces human error, especially in data processing, communication, and content generation.
- **Cost efficiency** : Automating workflows with GPT can lower operational costs by reducing the need for additional staff to manage routine tasks.
- **Scalability** : Businesses can handle increasing workloads without proportional increases in staff, thanks to GPT-driven automation tools.
- **Improved customer experience** : GPT can power chatbots and automated support systems, providing quick and accurate responses, improving overall customer satisfaction.

Practical Tips to Maximise Earnings from Automating Workflows with GPT

1. **Identify repetitive tasks** : Start by identifying areas where GPT can automate time-consuming tasks like drafting emails, creating reports, or generating social media content.
2. **Offer custom solutions** : Provide tailored GPT-based automation tools that fit the specific needs of different businesses, such as automating HR processes, customer interactions, or marketing activities.
3. **Provide ongoing support** : Offer a subscription or retainer model for businesses needing regular updates, training, and troubleshooting as they incorporate GPT into their workflows.
4. **Implement AI-powered customer support** : Develop and integrate GPT-based chatbots to handle routine customer queries, allowing businesses to scale customer service operations without adding extra personnel.
5. **Use GPT for content automation** : GPT can be employed to automatically generate content for blogs, emails, reports, and product descriptions, saving businesses significant time and resources.

Example: GPT for HR Workflow Automation

For a company looking to automate its HR processes:

- **Resume screening** : GPT can be used to scan and rank CVs based on job requirements, reducing the time spent manually reviewing applications.
- **Employee onboarding** : Automate communication with new hires by generating onboarding emails, training schedules, and policy documents using GPT.
- **Performance review assistance** : GPT can draft performance review summaries based on predefined metrics, helping HR teams streamline the evaluation process.

Resources to Help Automate Business Workflows with GPT

- **Zapier** : A workflow automation tool that can be integrated with GPT to create custom workflows that handle repetitive tasks.

- **OpenAI API** : Offers direct access to GPT models for businesses to integrate AI into their custom applications and workflows.
- **Integromat (Make)** : Another automation platform that can be linked with GPT to automate business processes across apps and tools.
- **HubSpot** : A CRM platform where GPT can be integrated to automate customer communications and lead generation processes.
- **Trello or Asana** : Use GPT to automate project management workflows, such as creating task lists, updating progress reports, and sending reminders.

Maximising Earnings from GPT Workflow Automation

1. **Create automation packages** : Offer businesses a range of automation services, from customer support to content creation, with GPT-driven workflows, creating custom packages that meet their needs.
2. **Develop GPT-powered SaaS solutions** : Build software-as-a-service (SaaS) platforms powered by GPT, allowing businesses to automate specific tasks like

generating reports, creating content, or managing customer support.

3. **Consultancy services** : Provide consulting on how businesses can integrate GPT into their existing systems, offering bespoke solutions to optimise workflows and increase efficiency.

4. **Offer training programmes** : Provide training to businesses on how to implement and use GPT tools effectively, creating an additional revenue stream.

5. **Collaborate with tech agencies** : Partner with tech or digital agencies to integrate GPT into their client solutions, enabling them to offer advanced automation as part of their service.

Additional Revenue Streams

1. **GPT-powered chatbot creation** : Design and implement GPT-driven chatbots that handle customer inquiries, allowing businesses to improve customer service while reducing operational costs.

2. **Automated report generation** : Offer services where GPT automatically generates business reports based on

specific metrics, allowing companies to save time on data analysis and reporting.

3. **Custom AI integration services** : Assist businesses in integrating GPT with their existing tools and software, providing a seamless workflow automation experience.

4. **Create templates** : Develop and sell ready-made automation templates using GPT for specific business functions such as customer service, sales follow-ups, and email marketing campaigns.

5. **Affiliate marketing** : Promote GPT-based tools and platforms (like OpenAI API integrations) through affiliate marketing, earning commissions on successful referrals.

Leveraging GPT for Workflow Automation

1. **Automating email communication** : GPT can automate email generation, whether for marketing campaigns, internal updates, or customer queries. Tools like **ActiveCampaign** or **Mailchimp** can be integrated with GPT for seamless email automation.

2. **Data-driven decision-making** : GPT can be used to process and summarise large sets

of data, offering insights that help businesses make more informed decisions without manual analysis.

3. **Marketing automation** : Use GPT to automate marketing tasks such as creating personalised social media posts, writing product descriptions, or generating blog content that aligns with SEO goals.

4. **AI-powered task management** : Automate project management workflows by using GPT to create task lists, update team members on progress, and suggest priority actions based on deadlines.

5. **Customer engagement** : GPT can be used to automatically generate follow-up emails or messages, keeping customers engaged and improving retention without manual effort.

Maximising Success with GPT Automation

- **Focus on ROI** : Ensure businesses understand the cost savings and productivity boosts they can achieve with GPT automation. Emphasise how automating repetitive tasks can free up resources for more strategic work.

- **Customise solutions** : Offer tailored automation solutions that align with the specific needs and goals of each business. This increases the likelihood of adoption and client satisfaction.
- **Regular updates and innovation** : The AI space evolves quickly. Stay up-to-date with the latest advancements in GPT technology to provide cutting-edge solutions that offer continuous improvement to workflows.
- **Emphasise human oversight** : While GPT can automate many processes, human oversight is still necessary to ensure that the content, decisions, or actions generated align with the business's values and objectives.

By offering GPT-based workflow automation, you can provide businesses with a competitive edge by improving their efficiency and productivity. With an understanding of how to integrate GPT effectively into various business processes, you can establish a valuable service that drives both client success and your own earnings potential.

Chapter 34
Generating Stock Market Analysis Reports

Using GPT technology to generate stock market analysis reports provides financial professionals, traders, and investors with a fast, reliable, and data-driven approach to analysing market trends, company performance, and investment opportunities. GPT models can process large volumes of financial data, offering insights that would otherwise require significant time and effort to compile manually. This summary provides practical tips, examples, and resources to help you maximise your earning potential by generating stock market analysis reports with GPT.

Importance of Automating Stock Market Analysis

- **Data-driven insights** : GPT can quickly analyse and summarise vast amounts of financial data, delivering actionable insights in real time.
- **Timely reports** : Automation enables quick generation of reports, helping investors stay ahead of market trends and act on opportunities.
- **Consistency and accuracy** : GPT minimises human error in interpreting data

and provides consistent analysis across reports.

- **Customisable reports** : Reports can be tailored to specific needs, whether focusing on individual stocks, sectors, or broader market trends.
- **Increased productivity** : Automating report generation frees financial analysts to focus on higher-level strategy and decision-making.

Practical Tips to Maximise Earnings from GPT-Generated Stock Market Reports

1. **Offer custom report services** : Provide bespoke stock analysis reports for individual clients or firms, tailored to their investment preferences and strategies.
2. **Leverage real-time data** : Integrate GPT with APIs that provide real-time stock market data, ensuring that your reports are always up-to-date.
3. **Expand into niche markets** : Specialise in specific industries or market sectors, offering in-depth, tailored analysis that appeals to specialised traders or investors.
4. **Create subscription-based services** : Offer daily, weekly, or monthly stock market

analysis reports to clients through a subscription model, providing a steady income stream.

5. **Combine with technical analysis** : Use GPT to not only summarise market news but also to generate reports that combine technical analysis indicators like moving averages, RSI, or MACD to offer deeper insights.

6. **Offer alerts and recommendations** : Use GPT to create automatic alerts for clients when key financial events occur or when stock prices meet predetermined thresholds.

Example: GPT-Generated Stock Analysis Report

A sample GPT-generated stock market report might include:

- **Market overview** : A summary of the day's market performance, highlighting major movements in key indices like the FTSE 100 or S&P 500.
- **Stock performance** : Detailed analysis of specific stocks based on current prices, volume, and recent news.
- **Technical analysis** : Interpretation of stock charts and indicators such as trend lines,

moving averages, or support and resistance levels.

- **Company fundamentals** : Summaries of earnings reports, profit margins, and other key financial ratios for individual companies.
- **Sector analysis** : An in-depth look at how different industries are performing in the current market environment, highlighting growth or risk factors.
- **Investment recommendations** : Buy, sell, or hold suggestions based on the data analysis and overall market outlook.

Resources to Help with Stock Market Report Generation

- **Yahoo Finance API** : Use this API to gather real-time stock market data for analysis in your GPT-driven reports.
- **Alpha Vantage API** : Another powerful API that offers detailed financial data, including stock prices, historical data, and company performance metrics.
- **TradingView** : A popular platform that provides a wealth of charting tools and technical analysis indicators, which can complement your GPT-generated reports.

- **QuantConnect** : A backtesting and algorithmic trading platform that can be integrated with GPT models to help validate stock analysis and predictions.
- **Bloomberg Terminal** : Though premium, this resource provides in-depth financial news and data that can be used in conjunction with GPT to generate high-quality reports.

Maximising Earnings from Stock Market Analysis Reports

1. **Develop a premium product** : Offer in-depth, high-quality reports that include both fundamental and technical analysis. This type of report could be offered to institutional investors, hedge funds, or high-net-worth individuals at a premium price.
2. **Monetise through financial institutions** : Partner with banks, brokerage firms, or investment platforms to offer GPT-driven stock analysis reports to their clients, either as part of their investment tools or as a separate service.
3. **Sell to retail investors** : Offer affordable, easy-to-understand reports for individual

investors looking for guidance on their portfolio. This could include beginner-friendly analysis or more sophisticated options for experienced traders.

4. **Affiliate marketing** : Promote stock market tools, platforms, or brokerages through your reports and earn commissions through affiliate marketing.

5. **Build AI-driven investment tools** : Create applications that generate live stock market reports for users, providing them with automated market insights and earning potential through subscription fees or advertising.

Additional Revenue Streams

1. **Stock market newsletter** : Launch a newsletter offering daily or weekly stock analysis reports generated with GPT. Monetise through subscriptions or sponsorships.

2. **Consulting services** : Offer one-on-one consulting for clients who need more personalised or bespoke stock market analysis services. You can combine your financial expertise with GPT-driven insights to provide comprehensive support.

3. **Automated investment suggestions** : Use GPT to create a tool that suggests trades or investment strategies based on real-time data, offering users an AI-powered trading assistant.
4. **Training and courses** : Develop online courses that teach traders and investors how to use AI-generated stock reports effectively. Offer these courses through platforms like Udemy or Teachable.
5. **AI-powered stock alerts** : Sell access to a service that sends real-time stock alerts based on market movements, GPT-generated analysis, or specific financial indicators.

Leveraging GPT for Stock Market Report Generation

1. **Automated earnings summaries** : Use GPT to quickly summarise company earnings reports, highlighting key financials such as revenue, profit, and earnings per share. This can save investors hours of analysis time.
2. **Analysing market sentiment** : GPT can scan financial news, social media, and other data sources to determine market sentiment

for specific stocks or sectors, providing valuable context for investment decisions.

3. **Predictive analysis** : While GPT cannot predict the future with certainty, it can process historical data to identify trends or patterns that may indicate future market movements.

4. **Risk analysis** : Use GPT to generate risk assessments for various stocks or portfolios by analysing factors such as market volatility, sector performance, and macroeconomic indicators.

5. **Automate compliance reports** : For financial institutions, GPT can automate the generation of compliance reports by summarising and organising regulatory updates and requirements.

Maximising Success with GPT Stock Market Reports

- **Stay informed** : Keep your GPT models updated with the latest financial data and trends to ensure your reports are accurate and relevant.
- **Customise for the audience** : Tailor your reports based on the experience level of your clients. For retail investors, simplify complex financial terms. For institutional

clients, include advanced analytics and detailed data.

- **Combine GPT with human expertise** : While GPT can automate much of the report generation process, human oversight ensures that the analysis is accurate and aligned with client goals.
- **Focus on timely delivery** : Ensure your GPT-powered reports are generated and delivered promptly, allowing investors to act quickly on the insights provided.
- **Offer multilingual reports** : Use GPT to generate stock market analysis reports in multiple languages, catering to international clients and broadening your customer base.

By integrating GPT into stock market analysis report generation, you can provide valuable insights to investors, traders, and financial institutions. With the right tools, strategies, and offerings, this service can be a significant revenue stream that enhances both your business and your clients' financial success.

Chapter 35
Producing AI-Powered Financial Newsletters

AI-powered financial newsletters offer a modern, efficient way to deliver curated, data-driven financial news, insights, and investment tips to subscribers. Using GPT technology, you can create personalised and highly informative newsletters that cater to different investment interests, providing timely market updates, stock analysis, and economic news. This summary includes practical tips, examples, and resources to help you maximise your earning potential by producing AI-powered financial newsletters.

Importance of AI-Powered Financial Newsletters

- **Automation of content** : GPT can automatically generate financial insights, reducing the manual effort required to produce regular, high-quality content.
- **Timeliness** : AI-powered tools can access and summarise real-time financial data, delivering up-to-the-minute market news to your subscribers.
- **Personalisation** : You can tailor content to the specific needs and preferences of your audience, whether they are retail investors, traders, or financial professionals.

- **Cost-effective** : Automating content creation with AI allows you to produce newsletters at scale, enabling you to reach more readers without the need for large editorial teams.
- **Scalability** : As your subscriber base grows, AI-powered newsletters can easily accommodate the increased demand without compromising on quality or speed.

Practical Tips to Maximise Earnings from AI-Powered Financial Newsletters

1. **Identify your target audience** : Tailor your newsletter content to specific types of investors or financial professionals. For example, focus on beginner investors, day traders, or wealth managers to ensure your content is relevant and valuable.
2. **Offer different subscription tiers** : Provide free newsletters with basic information, while offering premium tiers for subscribers who want in-depth market analysis, stock picks, or investment strategies.
3. **Focus on niche markets** : Cater to specific financial sectors, such as cryptocurrency, sustainable investing, or emerging markets,

to differentiate your newsletter from general financial news sources.

4. **Monetise with advertisements** : Once your newsletter gains a substantial following, attract sponsorships or include ads from financial institutions, brokerages, or fintech companies.

5. **Integrate expert analysis** : Use GPT to generate basic insights, and combine them with expert commentary to add value and establish credibility.

6. **Create exclusive content** : Offer special reports or weekly stock picks that are only available to paying subscribers, increasing the perceived value of your newsletter.

Example: AI-Powered Financial Newsletter Format

A typical GPT-driven financial newsletter might include:

- **Market overview** : A brief summary of the day's financial markets, including major stock indices, bond yields, and commodities like oil or gold.
- **Stock highlights** : AI-generated analysis of top-performing or underperforming stocks, based on real-time data.

- **Investment tips** : Short insights on potential stock buys or sectors to watch, personalised for different types of investors (e.g., long-term investors or day traders).
- **Economic updates** : Summaries of major economic reports, such as GDP growth, inflation data, or central bank interest rate decisions.
- **Upcoming events** : Alerts for upcoming earnings reports, government policy announcements, or significant financial events that could impact the market.
- **Expert commentary** : If desired, combine AI-generated content with human analysis or expert opinions to give your newsletter a more personalised and authoritative tone.

Resources to Help Produce AI-Powered Financial Newsletters

- **OpenAI API** : Use GPT to generate high-quality content for your newsletter, from stock analysis to market summaries.
- **Yahoo Finance API** : Access real-time financial data, including stock prices, news updates, and market trends, to feed into your AI-powered newsletter.

- **Alpha Vantage API** : Another great source of financial data, offering stock, forex, and cryptocurrency information for inclusion in your newsletter.
- **Substack** : A popular platform for launching paid newsletters, Substack allows you to build a subscription-based audience for your financial content.
- **Mailchimp** : Use this email marketing platform to automate newsletter distribution and manage your subscriber list effectively.

Maximising Earnings from AI-Powered Financial Newsletters

1. **Create a freemium model** : Offer a free version of your newsletter to attract readers, then upsell premium content such as exclusive stock tips or in-depth market analysis.
2. **Affiliate marketing** : Partner with financial services, such as online trading platforms or investment courses, and promote them in your newsletter. Earn commissions on sales or referrals.
3. **Premium consultancy** : In addition to your newsletter, offer one-on-one consultations

or premium investment research reports for a fee, allowing subscribers to access deeper financial advice.

4. **Group subscription deals** : Partner with financial institutions or investment clubs to offer your newsletter as part of their subscription services or benefits to their clients.

5. **Host webinars** : Offer subscribers exclusive access to webinars where you delve deeper into financial topics or provide live stock market analysis, creating additional revenue streams.

Additional Revenue Streams

1. **Sponsorship deals** : As your newsletter grows in popularity, you can partner with financial companies or fintech startups for paid sponsorship deals, showcasing their products or services to your readers.

2. **Exclusive reports** : Use GPT to generate special reports on specific financial topics, like sector analysis, market predictions, or investment strategies, and sell these as standalone products.

3. **Partnerships with financial influencers** : Collaborate with well-known finance

bloggers or social media influencers to co-promote your newsletter, helping you grow your audience and monetise through partnerships.

4. **Financial training courses** : Create and sell online courses that teach subscribers how to make sense of financial data, use AI tools for investing, or improve their financial literacy.

5. **Data-driven insights for institutions** : Offer a premium service where you generate in-depth, data-driven insights using GPT for financial institutions, hedge funds, or wealth managers.

Leveraging AI to Enhance Newsletter Content

1. **Personalisation at scale** : GPT allows you to create personalised content for different audience segments, providing each reader with stock recommendations or analysis based on their interests or risk tolerance.

2. **Sentiment analysis** : Use GPT to perform sentiment analysis on financial news and social media, providing your readers with insights into market trends and investor sentiment.

3. **Multilingual capabilities** : Expand your audience by offering newsletters in multiple languages, using GPT's language generation capabilities to automatically translate and adapt content for international markets.
4. **Automate stock recommendations** : With real-time data inputs, GPT can generate stock recommendations based on technical indicators, company performance, and market trends, offering your subscribers actionable investment insights.
5. **Enhanced readability** : Use GPT to summarise complex financial reports, making them accessible and digestible for a wider audience, especially for retail investors who may not have in-depth financial knowledge.

Maximising Success with AI-Powered Financial Newsletters

- **Deliver value consistently** : Ensure your newsletters provide actionable insights and valuable information that subscribers can rely on for their investment decisions. The more value you offer, the higher your subscriber retention rate will be.

- **Refine content based on feedback** : Use subscriber feedback and data analytics to continuously refine and improve the content, format, and delivery of your newsletters.
- **Stay up-to-date with financial trends** : Ensure that your GPT models are regularly updated with the latest financial news and trends to provide accurate and timely analysis.
- **Focus on building trust** : Establish your credibility by blending AI-generated insights with human expertise. Offering thoughtful, balanced financial advice will help you build long-term relationships with your audience.
- **Diversify your offerings** : To maximise earnings, consider expanding beyond newsletters into other financial content, such as market reports, e-books, or live seminars.

By producing AI-powered financial newsletters, you can create a scalable and profitable business that delivers valuable market insights to a broad range of investors. With the right blend of automation, personalisation, and financial expertise, you can offer a product that drives both subscriber growth and revenue.

Chapter 36

Offering Custom AI Chatbot Development

Custom AI chatbot development is a lucrative service that enables businesses to automate customer interactions, improve user engagement, and streamline internal processes. By offering AI-powered chatbot solutions, you can help clients enhance customer service, boost sales, and increase productivity. This summary provides practical tips, examples, and resources to help you maximise your earning potential in the chatbot development field.

Importance of Custom AI Chatbot Development

- **24/7 Availability** : AI chatbots can operate round the clock, handling customer queries at any time without the need for human agents.
- **Scalability** : Chatbots can manage multiple conversations simultaneously, making them ideal for businesses with high volumes of customer interactions.
- **Cost-Effective** : Automating routine customer service tasks can reduce staffing costs, while still offering quick and efficient support.

- **Improved Customer Experience** : AI-powered chatbots can provide personalised responses, improving customer satisfaction by delivering relevant information or solutions.
- **Data Collection and Insights** : Chatbots can collect valuable customer data, which businesses can use to enhance products, services, and marketing strategies.

Practical Tips to Maximise Earnings from AI Chatbot Development

1. **Identify Target Industries** : Focus on industries that benefit the most from AI chatbot technology, such as e-commerce, finance, healthcare, and real estate. Each of these sectors has specific use cases for chatbots, including customer support, lead generation, and appointment scheduling.
2. **Offer Customised Solutions** : Create chatbots tailored to the specific needs of each client, such as sales chatbots, customer support bots, or internal workflow automation bots. A customised approach allows you to charge premium prices.

3. **Leverage NLP (Natural Language Processing)** : Ensure your chatbots are equipped with advanced NLP to understand customer queries better and deliver more accurate, human-like responses.
4. **Integrate with Business Systems** : Offer chatbots that can integrate with popular CRM systems (e.g., Salesforce, HubSpot), e-commerce platforms (e.g., Shopify, WooCommerce), and communication tools (e.g., Slack, Microsoft Teams), enhancing their functionality and usability.
5. **Offer a Subscription Model** : Provide ongoing chatbot maintenance, updates, and analytics as part of a subscription package, creating a steady revenue stream.
6. **Incorporate Multilingual Capabilities** : Develop chatbots that can communicate in multiple languages to serve a broader, global audience and attract international clients.

Example Use Cases of Custom AI Chatbots

- **E-commerce Support** : Chatbots can assist online shoppers by recommending products, answering questions about pricing, or processing returns.

- **Healthcare Appointment Scheduling** : Chatbots can manage patient appointment bookings, send reminders, and answer frequently asked questions about services or medical conditions.
- **Banking and Finance** : Chatbots can help customers check account balances, transfer funds, or answer questions about financial products, all within a secure framework.
- **Real Estate** : Chatbots can qualify leads by asking potential buyers questions about their preferences and connecting them with real estate agents when appropriate.

Resources to Help Develop Custom AI Chatbots

- **Dialogflow** : A platform by Google for building conversational interfaces. It integrates with popular messaging platforms like Facebook Messenger and Slack and offers pre-built templates for various industries.
- **Microsoft Bot Framework** : A tool for creating, testing, and deploying intelligent bots across different channels such as websites, apps, and social media platforms.

- **Rasa** : An open-source AI platform that allows you to build custom, on-premise chatbots with advanced NLP capabilities. It's ideal for businesses that require high levels of data privacy.
- **Chatfuel** : A user-friendly platform for developing chatbots without coding. It's widely used for creating Facebook Messenger bots and is suited to smaller businesses or startups.
- **IBM Watson Assistant** : A powerful AI tool that offers pre-built industry models and allows the development of highly customisable chatbots with machine learning capabilities.

Maximising Earnings from Custom AI Chatbot Development

1. **Offer End-to-End Solutions** : Provide a complete service that includes chatbot design, development, deployment, and ongoing support. Clients are more likely to pay a premium for a full solution rather than a piecemeal approach.
2. **Develop Industry-Specific Chatbots** : Specialise in chatbots for specific sectors,

such as healthcare or retail, where the need for automation and customer interaction is high. Customising bots for niche markets allows you to charge more for your services.

3. **Monetise via SaaS** : Offer your chatbot services as a SaaS (Software as a Service) model, allowing businesses to subscribe to chatbot hosting, updates, and performance monitoring on a recurring basis.

4. **Upsell Analytics Services** : Offer advanced analytics as an additional service, providing businesses with insights into chatbot performance, customer behaviour, and conversion rates.

5. **Develop Chatbot Templates** : Create chatbot templates for specific industries or use cases and sell these as one-time products or through a licensing model. This can help you earn passive income while focusing on custom projects.

Additional Revenue Streams

1. **White-Label Chatbots** : Develop white-label chatbots for other digital agencies or businesses that can rebrand and resell them to their clients.

2. **Training and Consulting** : Offer training or consulting services to businesses that want to manage their chatbots in-house. This can be an additional revenue stream on top of development services.
3. **API Integration** : Offer custom chatbot solutions that integrate with third-party services, such as customer relationship management (CRM) software, payment systems, and marketing automation platforms.
4. **Create Plugins or Extensions** : Develop and sell plugins or extensions that enhance existing chatbot platforms, such as adding payment gateways, language translation, or advanced analytics tools.
5. **Chatbot Maintenance and Optimisation** : Provide ongoing support and optimisation services for your clients' chatbots. This includes monitoring performance, troubleshooting, and implementing updates to improve accuracy and efficiency.

Leveraging AI to Enhance Chatbot Capabilities

1. **AI-Driven Personalisation** : Use GPT to create chatbots that learn from past

interactions to deliver more personalised recommendations and responses based on individual user preferences and behaviour.

2. **Sentiment Analysis** : Incorporate sentiment analysis to allow your chatbot to understand the emotional tone of customer queries and adjust its responses accordingly, improving user experience.

3. **Automated Customer Segmentation** : Chatbots can automatically segment customers based on their interactions, allowing businesses to target them with more relevant marketing or product recommendations.

4. **Voice Recognition and Assistance** : Build chatbots that support voice commands and integrate with voice assistants like Amazon Alexa or Google Assistant, offering users a more dynamic interaction experience.

5. **Task Automation** : Develop chatbots that not only respond to queries but also automate internal tasks, such as booking appointments, generating invoices, or updating CRM systems.

Maximising Success with Custom AI Chatbot Development

- **Test for User Experience** : Continuously test and improve your chatbots to ensure they deliver smooth, accurate, and helpful user interactions. The better the user experience, the more likely businesses will see value in your solutions.
- **Educate Clients** : Provide clients with comprehensive training on how to use and maximise the capabilities of their AI-powered chatbots. This can enhance the long-term success of the chatbot and lead to repeat business.
- **Focus on Security** : Ensure that your chatbots, especially those handling sensitive information like in banking or healthcare, comply with industry security standards, such as GDPR or HIPAA.
- **Stay Updated** : Keep up with the latest advancements in AI, machine learning, and NLP to continually improve your chatbot solutions and stay ahead of competitors.
- **Promote Multichannel Integration** : Ensure your chatbots can seamlessly interact with users across various platforms, such as websites, mobile apps, and social

media, to create a cohesive customer experience.

By offering custom AI chatbot development services, you can tap into a growing market and provide businesses with tools that improve efficiency and customer engagement. With the right approach, tools, and business model, you can maximise your earning potential while delivering value to your clients.

Chapter 37
Building Niche Affiliate Marketing Websites

Niche affiliate marketing websites focus on a specific topic, product category, or interest, allowing you to earn commissions by promoting affiliate products. These websites are designed to attract a targeted audience, providing useful information and reviews that lead visitors to purchase through your affiliate links. By narrowing down on a niche, you can create highly focused content that resonates with a specific demographic, boosting conversion rates and earnings. This summary includes practical tips, examples, and resources to help you maximise your earning potential in building niche affiliate marketing websites.

Importance of Niche Affiliate Marketing Websites

- **Higher Conversion Rates** : Focusing on a specific niche allows you to target a more interested audience, increasing the likelihood of conversions.
- **Less Competition** : Compared to broader categories, niche markets often have fewer competitors, giving you a better chance to rank higher in search engine results.
- **Authority and Trust** : A specialised website helps you position yourself as an expert in your chosen niche, increasing trust and credibility with your audience.
- **Long-Term Income** : Affiliate marketing websites, once established, can generate passive income over time as long as you continue to drive traffic and conversions.

Practical Tips to Maximise Earnings from Niche Affiliate Marketing Websites

1. **Choose the Right Niche** : Select a niche that balances passion, profitability, and market demand. Look for niches where there are enough products to promote and

where people are actively searching for solutions or reviews online.

- **Example niches** : Health supplements, eco-friendly products, gaming accessories, pet supplies, or home fitness equipment.

2. **Research Affiliate Programs** : Partner with affiliate programs that offer competitive commission rates and high-quality products. Platforms like Amazon Associates, ShareASale, and Commission Junction provide access to a wide variety of products across different niches.

3. **Create High-Quality Content** : Write detailed reviews, how-to guides, and comparison articles that offer real value to your visitors. Focus on addressing common questions or problems your audience may have, and recommend products that can solve these issues.

4. **Optimise for SEO** : Ensure your website is optimised for search engines. Use keyword research tools like Ahrefs, SEMrush, or Google Keyword Planner to identify relevant keywords for your niche and create content around them.

5. **Use Content Marketing** : In addition to SEO, promote your content through social media, email marketing, and forums where your target audience is active. Creating useful and shareable content can drive organic traffic to your site.
6. **Diversify Revenue Streams** : In addition to affiliate commissions, consider adding other monetisation methods like Google AdSense, sponsored content, or selling digital products (e-books, online courses) related to your niche.
7. **Leverage Data Analytics** : Use tools like Google Analytics to track traffic sources, user behaviour, and conversion rates. This data will help you refine your content and marketing strategies to maximise earnings.

Example: Niche Affiliate Marketing Website Structure

A well-structured affiliate marketing website typically includes:

- **Home Page** : A clear, informative introduction to your niche, with featured product reviews or guides.

- **Product Reviews** : Detailed reviews of individual products, including pros and cons, user experiences, and affiliate links to buy the product.
- **Comparison Articles** : Content that compares similar products to help visitors make informed decisions, with links to the best-rated or most popular options.
- **How-To Guides** : Instructional articles that educate your audience about your niche topic while subtly recommending affiliate products as solutions.
- **Blog Section** : Regularly updated blog posts discussing trends, tips, or personal stories related to the niche, driving engagement and SEO.

Resources to Help Build Niche Affiliate Marketing Websites

- **WordPress** : The most popular platform for building affiliate marketing websites, offering themes and plugins that simplify the process.
- **Elementor** : A drag-and-drop website builder for WordPress that allows you to

create professional-looking pages without coding.

- **SEMrush** : An SEO tool that helps with keyword research, competitor analysis, and on-page SEO optimisation.
- **Astra Theme** : A fast, lightweight WordPress theme designed for SEO and perfect for building niche affiliate sites.
- **Affiliate Plugins** : Tools like ThirstyAffiliates or Pretty Links that allow you to manage and cloak your affiliate links easily, making them look clean and professional.

Maximising Earnings from Niche Affiliate Marketing Websites

1. **Target Long-Tail Keywords** : These are highly specific search queries that usually have lower competition but higher intent. For example, instead of targeting "fitness equipment," you might focus on "best adjustable dumbbells for small spaces."
2. **Build an Email List** : Capture emails by offering a free resource, such as an e-book or discount code, related to your niche. Use email marketing to send subscribers product recommendations, content updates, and special offers.

3. **Test and Optimise CTAs** : Experiment with different types of calls-to-action (CTAs) for your affiliate links. For example, "Buy Now," "See Price on Amazon," or "Check Reviews" can have different effects on conversion rates.
4. **Regularly Update Content** : Refresh older articles to keep them relevant and up to date. This can improve your SEO rankings and ensure you are recommending the latest and most relevant products in your niche.
5. **Leverage Social Proof** : Include customer reviews or testimonials within your product reviews to build trust and encourage conversions.

Additional Revenue Streams

1. **E-books and Courses** : Once you've established yourself as an authority in your niche, create and sell e-books or online courses that provide in-depth knowledge or tutorials.
2. **Sponsored Posts** : Partner with brands in your niche to create sponsored content. This

could be in the form of product reviews, tutorials, or dedicated blog posts.

3. **Membership Site** : Offer exclusive content, guides, or personalised advice for a monthly fee. This creates a recurring revenue stream alongside affiliate commissions.

4. **Influencer Collaborations** : As your website gains traffic and credibility, brands may approach you for partnerships. You can collaborate with influencers in your niche to promote products and earn commissions.

5. **YouTube or Video Content** : Complement your website with a YouTube channel where you review products or create how-to guides, linking back to your affiliate website.

Leveraging AI and Automation for Affiliate Marketing Success

1. **AI Content Generation** : Tools like GPT-powered content generators can help you produce product reviews, articles, and guides quickly, allowing you to scale content production.

2. **Chatbots for User Engagement** : Implement AI chatbots on your site to help visitors find products, answer questions, or

recommend relevant affiliate links based on their preferences.

3. **Automated Email Marketing** : Use platforms like Mailchimp or ConvertKit to automate email marketing campaigns, sending affiliate promotions or new content updates to your subscribers.

Maximising Success with Niche Affiliate Marketing Websites

- **Focus on User Intent** : Understand what your audience is looking for when they visit your website and provide content that solves their problems or answers their questions, while naturally recommending affiliate products.
- **Diversify Traffic Sources** : Don't rely solely on SEO. Use social media, paid advertising, and email marketing to drive traffic to your site.
- **Prioritise Mobile Optimisation** : Ensure your website is mobile-friendly, as more people are shopping and browsing on mobile devices. A responsive design improves user experience and can boost conversion rates.

- **Build Trust with Your Audience** : Be transparent about your affiliate partnerships. Offer genuine, unbiased reviews and avoid over-promoting products. This builds credibility and long-term trust with your readers.
- **Scale Strategically** : Once your first niche site is generating steady income, consider building additional niche websites in other profitable markets to diversify your revenue streams.

By building niche affiliate marketing websites, you can tap into targeted markets, providing valuable content that leads to conversions and commissions. With the right strategy, tools, and consistent effort, niche affiliate marketing websites can become a significant source of passive income.

Chapter 38
Developing AI-Generated Fiction Stories

AI-generated fiction is an emerging and innovative way to produce creative stories using artificial intelligence tools like GPT. By leveraging AI, writers and content creators can develop engaging fiction across various genres, from short stories to full-length novels, with speed and efficiency. This approach can help aspiring writers produce content faster and allow professionals to experiment with new ideas and formats. In this summary, you will find practical tips, examples, and resources to help maximise your earning potential in AI-generated fiction.

Importance of AI-Generated Fiction Stories

- **Increased Productivity** : AI can generate story ideas, outlines, or even entire chapters, speeding up the writing process and helping authors create more content in less time.
- **Creative Inspiration** : AI-generated prompts and story suggestions can help overcome writer's block and inspire new and unique narratives.
- **Scalability** : AI allows authors to scale their fiction output, catering to diverse audiences and genres, making it easier to publish more frequently.
- **Accessibility for New Writers** : Even those with little experience in writing can use AI tools to create publishable fiction, lowering

the barrier to entry in the creative writing field.

Practical Tips to Maximise Earnings from AI-Generated Fiction Stories

1. **Select a Target Genre** : Choose a genre that has demand in the market. Popular genres for AI-generated fiction include science fiction, fantasy, romance, and mystery. Each of these genres has an established audience, making it easier to find readers.
2. **Use AI for Story Outlines and Plotting** : AI tools can generate detailed outlines based on a few prompts or ideas. This helps in planning the structure of a story, allowing writers to focus on refining characters, dialogue, and themes.

   - **Example** : Input basic elements such as "space exploration," "alien civilisation," and "conflict over resources," and AI can generate a complete plot outline for a science fiction story.

3. **Collaborate with AI for Character Development** : Use AI to generate character backstories, motivations, and personality traits. This can help ensure that characters are well-rounded and consistent throughout the narrative.
4. **Automate World-Building** : AI can assist in creating detailed settings for fantasy or sci-fi stories, generating descriptions of fictional worlds, societies, and ecosystems that can add depth to the narrative.
5. **Use AI for Dialogue and Prose** : AI tools like GPT can be used to create natural-sounding dialogue or descriptive passages. This helps when you need to quickly draft sections of a story, which you can later refine and personalise.
6. **Edit and Proofread Manually** : While AI can generate content, it's essential to review and edit the output to ensure coherence, tone, and style match your vision. Manual editing ensures the AI-generated text feels human and avoids repetitive or awkward phrasing.
7. **Publish Frequently** : AI allows for faster production of content, enabling you to publish short stories, serialised fiction, or even full-length books at a higher frequency.

This can help you build a consistent readership.

Example Use Case: AI-Generated Fiction for Self-Publishing

Many authors are turning to self-publishing platforms like Amazon Kindle Direct Publishing (KDP) to publish AI-generated fiction. By producing niche genre fiction, such as paranormal romance or post-apocalyptic adventures, authors can quickly build a catalogue of stories that cater to specific reader preferences.

Resources to Help Develop AI-Generated Fiction Stories

- **OpenAI's GPT** : A powerful AI language model that can generate fiction stories, outlines, and character descriptions based on prompts.
- **Sudowrite** : An AI tool designed specifically for fiction writers. It assists with brainstorming, writing, and refining stories, making it ideal for developing plots, settings, and characters.

- **Writesonic** : A versatile AI writing tool that helps create story ideas, plot summaries, and long-form fiction. It's useful for generating full narratives and automating repetitive tasks like dialogue or world-building.
- **NovelAI** : An AI tool that specialises in generating text for creative writing, particularly in genres like fantasy and science fiction. It provides features like lore generation and AI-assisted prose, perfect for long-form storytelling.
- **Scrivener** : A writing software that helps organise and manage long-form fiction. While not AI-powered, it is an essential tool for structuring novels and integrating AI-generated content into your workflow.

Maximising Earnings from AI-Generated Fiction

1. **Self-Publish E-books** : AI-generated fiction can be self-published on platforms like Amazon KDP, Smashwords, or Apple Books. By frequently releasing stories in popular genres, you can build a portfolio of works that generate passive income.

2. **Sell Short Stories** : Many platforms accept short stories for publication, including literary magazines, anthologies, and writing contests. AI can help you produce polished short stories quickly, increasing your chances of being published or winning prizes.

3. **Create Serialised Fiction** : Platforms like Wattpad and Radish allow writers to publish stories chapter by chapter. This model can attract loyal readers who are willing to pay for early access or premium content.

4. **Offer Ghostwriting Services** : Use AI to assist in ghostwriting fiction for clients who want to publish stories under their own names. Ghostwriting can be highly lucrative, particularly if you specialise in popular genres.

5. **Bundle Stories for Sales** : Group short stories or novellas into anthologies or collections to sell as complete works. Offering bundled content allows you to charge more and attract readers looking for value.

Additional Revenue Streams

1. **Patreon or Membership Platforms** : Offer exclusive access to AI-generated fiction, behind-the-scenes content, or early releases to subscribers on platforms like Patreon. This can create a recurring revenue stream from fans who support your work.
2. **Adaptation for Other Media** : AI-generated stories can be adapted into other formats like audiobooks, comics, or even film scripts. Partnering with voice actors or illustrators can help you tap into new markets.
3. **Collaborative Writing** : Partner with other authors or writing communities to co-write AI-generated fiction. Collaborative projects can expand your reach and introduce your work to new audiences.
4. **Offer AI Fiction Writing Workshops** : As AI-generated fiction becomes more popular, aspiring writers may be interested in learning how to use these tools. Offering workshops, courses, or tutorials on how to develop AI fiction can generate additional income.
5. **Monetise via Ad Revenue** : Publish AI-generated stories on your blog or website and monetise through ads, affiliate links, or sponsored content. This approach can help

diversify your income, especially as your readership grows.

Leveraging AI to Enhance Fiction Creation

1. **AI-Driven Personalisation** : Use AI to create personalised versions of stories for different readers. For example, offer readers the ability to choose different endings or alternate plot developments, increasing engagement and satisfaction.
2. **Collaborate with AI for Complex Plots** : Use AI to develop multi-layered plots with intricate twists and character arcs. AI can help track subplots and ensure consistency throughout a long-form story.
3. **Use AI for Genre Exploration** : Experiment with AI-generated fiction in different genres to find what resonates with your audience. By testing different genres, you can identify lucrative markets and niche opportunities.
4. **AI for Reader Interaction** : Develop interactive fiction using AI, where readers can influence the story's direction by making choices at key moments. This approach is especially appealing in digital formats and can enhance reader engagement.

Maximising Success with AI-Generated Fiction Stories

- **Focus on Quality** : While AI can generate large volumes of text quickly, it's essential to focus on quality. Spend time editing and refining the AI-generated content to ensure it meets the standards of your target audience.
- **Engage with Your Readers** : Build a community around your work by engaging with readers through social media, newsletters, or forums. Regularly interacting with your audience can help you gather feedback, improve your stories, and increase reader loyalty.
- **Develop a Strong Author Brand** : Whether writing under your own name or a pen name, create a consistent author brand that reflects the genres and themes you write in. This can help attract readers and build a following over time.
- **Test Different Formats** : AI-generated fiction can be published in various formats, from e-books to audiobooks and even interactive stories. Experiment with different formats to see what resonates with your audience and maximises your earnings.

- **Stay Updated on AI Advancements** : As AI technology evolves, new tools and capabilities will emerge. Keep up with the latest advancements in AI-generated content creation to improve your stories and maintain a competitive edge.

By developing AI-generated fiction stories, you can tap into a creative and fast-growing market. With the right tools, strategies, and attention to quality, AI-generated fiction can become a profitable and scalable venture.

Chapter 39
Creating AI-Powered Customer Surveys

AI-powered customer surveys offer businesses an efficient and scalable way to gather insights and feedback. Using AI tools like GPT, companies can create tailored surveys that are dynamic, personalised, and easy to analyse. By leveraging AI, survey creators can improve engagement, streamline data collection, and ensure that the feedback gathered is actionable. This summary explores practical tips, examples, and resources to help you maximise your earning potential by creating AI-powered customer surveys.

Importance of AI-Powered Customer Surveys

- **Personalisation** : AI allows for the creation of surveys that adapt based on customer responses, ensuring relevance and increasing completion rates.
- **Automation** : Automating the survey process reduces the time spent on designing questions, distributing surveys, and analysing responses, making it more efficient.
- **Data-Driven Insights** : AI tools can analyse large volumes of feedback to identify trends, customer sentiment, and actionable insights without manual input.
- **Scalability** : AI enables the creation of large-scale surveys that can be distributed to thousands of customers, all while maintaining personalisation and relevance.

Practical Tips to Maximise Earnings from AI-Powered Customer Surveys

1. **Define Your Target Audience** : Before creating a survey, understand who the target audience is and what specific insights you need from them. AI can help tailor

questions based on customer segments such as demographics, buying behaviour, or previous interactions.

- **Example** : A retail company might use AI to create personalised surveys for customers who have purchased specific products, asking targeted questions about their satisfaction with that item.

2. **Use Dynamic Questions** : AI can generate questions that change based on the respondent's previous answers. This dynamic approach makes surveys feel more conversational and less repetitive, improving the user experience and ensuring more accurate responses.

- **Example** : If a customer indicates dissatisfaction with a service, AI can automatically prompt follow-up questions to better understand the reason for the dissatisfaction.

3. **Leverage Natural Language Processing (NLP)** : NLP, a branch of AI, can help analyse open-ended responses by categorising feedback into themes,

sentiment, and actionable data. This removes the need for manual analysis, saving time and improving accuracy.
4. **Automate Survey Distribution** : AI can schedule surveys to be sent at optimal times based on customer behaviour, such as after a purchase or following customer support interactions. This ensures timely feedback while reducing manual intervention.
5. **Create Mobile-Friendly Surveys** : Ensure your surveys are optimised for mobile devices. AI tools can help generate mobile-responsive designs that improve engagement rates, particularly among on-the-go customers.
6. **Utilise AI for Predictive Analytics** : AI can predict customer behaviour based on survey responses, helping businesses anticipate future needs and tailor their offerings accordingly. This can lead to more proactive business strategies.

Example Use Case: AI-Powered Surveys for Customer Feedback

A SaaS company could use AI-powered surveys to gather customer feedback after users interact with their platform. AI could personalise questions based on user engagement, such as asking about ease of use for frequent users and suggesting feature improvements for less active users. AI would then analyse the feedback, allowing the company to prioritise product updates and improve user satisfaction.

Resources to Help Create AI-Powered Customer Surveys

- **Google Forms + GPT Integration** : Combine Google Forms with GPT to create AI-enhanced surveys that automatically generate questions and responses based on customer data.
- **Typeform** : An intuitive platform for creating engaging surveys, with AI capabilities to personalise survey questions and format.
- **SurveyMonkey** : A well-established survey tool that offers AI features like sentiment analysis and response prediction.
- **Qualtrics** : A professional platform for creating in-depth customer experience surveys, with AI-driven insights and advanced analytics.
- **Zapier** : Automate survey distribution and data collection by connecting AI survey tools

with business applications like CRM platforms or email marketing tools.

Maximising Earnings from AI-Powered Customer Surveys

1. **Offer Custom Survey Creation Services** : Businesses often need tailored surveys for customer feedback, product research, or employee engagement. By offering AI-powered survey creation as a service, you can charge a premium for surveys that deliver high-quality insights.
2. **Sell Data Insights** : Many companies struggle with analysing large volumes of survey data. Offer services that not only create the surveys but also use AI tools to provide detailed reports, highlighting trends, sentiments, and recommendations.
3. **Build Recurring Revenue** : Offer ongoing survey and data analysis services as a subscription. This could involve creating monthly or quarterly customer feedback surveys for businesses, along with regular reports on customer satisfaction and recommendations for improvement.
4. **Specialise in Niche Markets** : Focus on specific industries or sectors that require

regular feedback, such as e-commerce, healthcare, or hospitality. By becoming an expert in a niche, you can charge more for your specialised knowledge and services.

5. **Create AI-Driven Templates** : Develop a set of AI-generated survey templates for different industries or business needs. Sell these templates to companies or individuals looking to create their own surveys but lack the expertise to start from scratch.

6. **Monetise on Survey Platforms** : Create and sell high-quality survey templates or offer survey consulting services on platforms like Fiverr, Upwork, or Freelancer. Many businesses look for experts to help them design effective surveys.

Additional Revenue Streams

1. **Affiliate Marketing for Survey Tools** : Partner with AI survey platforms like Typeform, SurveyMonkey, or Qualtrics and earn commissions by recommending their services to clients who want to create their own surveys.

2. **Offer Training Workshops** : Create training materials or offer workshops on how to design and analyse AI-powered surveys.

This can appeal to businesses wanting to build internal expertise in using AI tools for customer feedback.

3. **Develop AI-Powered Chat Surveys** : Instead of traditional surveys, offer conversational chat surveys that use AI chatbots to engage customers. These chat-based surveys can be integrated into websites or apps for real-time feedback.

4. **Provide Feedback Loop Consulting** : Beyond survey creation, offer consulting on how businesses can act on survey data to close the feedback loop and improve customer satisfaction. This higher-level service adds significant value and can command higher fees.

Maximising Success with AI-Powered Customer Surveys

- **Focus on Engagement** : Ensure your surveys are interactive and engaging. Use AI to create questions that feel conversational and relevant to the respondent. Engaged participants are more likely to complete the survey and provide thoughtful responses.

- **Short and Simple** : AI can help keep surveys concise by asking only relevant questions, reducing survey fatigue and increasing completion rates.
- **Offer Incentives** : To boost response rates, consider offering rewards or incentives for completing surveys, such as discount codes or entry into prize draws. AI can automate the distribution of these rewards based on survey completion.
- **Analyse Trends Over Time** : Use AI to analyse how customer feedback evolves. This can help businesses identify long-term trends and make strategic adjustments based on customer sentiment.
- **Continuous Improvement** : Regularly update your surveys based on feedback and results. AI can suggest improvements to survey questions and formats, making them more effective over time.
- **A/B Testing with AI** : Experiment with different question formats and survey lengths using A/B testing. AI can quickly analyse which versions perform better, allowing you to optimise surveys for better engagement and insights.

By creating AI-powered customer surveys, you can provide businesses with valuable insights, improve customer engagement, and increase your own earning potential through a variety of revenue streams and services.

Chapter 40
Conducting AI-Assisted Market Research

AI-assisted market research combines the power of artificial intelligence with traditional research methods to deliver deeper insights and faster results. Using tools like GPT, businesses can gather and analyse vast amounts of data from multiple sources, gaining valuable market insights that would be difficult to achieve manually. This summary provides practical tips, examples, and resources to help you maximise your earning potential by offering AI-assisted market research services.

Importance of AI in Market Research

- **Efficiency** : AI automates data collection, analysis, and reporting, allowing businesses to access insights much faster than traditional methods.

- **Scalability** : AI enables the analysis of large datasets, including social media trends, consumer reviews, and competitor strategies, making it possible to conduct research on a large scale.
- **Accuracy** : AI-powered tools like GPT can identify patterns, trends, and insights that may be missed by human researchers, reducing the risk of bias and improving the accuracy of findings.
- **Real-time Insights** : AI tools can provide real-time data analysis, helping businesses stay ahead of market trends and make timely decisions.

Practical Tips for Conducting AI-Assisted Market Research

1. **Identify Key Research Objectives** : Before starting, clearly define the goals of your market research, whether it's to understand customer needs, track competitors, or assess market demand.

   - **Example** : A company might use AI to analyse social media conversations to understand customer sentiment towards a new product.

2. **Leverage Web Scraping Tools** : AI-powered web scraping tools can gather data from websites, social media platforms, and online forums. This data can then be analysed to uncover market trends and customer preferences.

   - **Example** : Use tools like ParseHub or Octoparse to collect customer reviews and product mentions across various platforms.

3. **Use Natural Language Processing (NLP) for Sentiment Analysis** : NLP, a key component of AI, can analyse text data to detect the tone and sentiment of customer reviews, social media posts, and feedback, helping businesses understand public opinion.

   - **Example** : Analyse thousands of social media posts to determine whether a product launch is being positively or negatively received.

4. **Automate Surveys and Polls** : AI can generate dynamic surveys that adapt based on responses, ensuring that the data collected is relevant and insightful. Automate the analysis of survey results for faster decision-making.

   - **Example** : Create a survey using AI to automatically adjust questions based on previous responses, improving data quality.

5. **Track Competitor Performance** : AI tools can track competitor pricing, product releases, and marketing campaigns, providing insights into competitor strategies and market positioning.

   - **Example** : Use AI to monitor competitor websites and social media activity for real-time updates on their latest promotions and customer interactions.

6. **Forecast Market Trends with Predictive Analytics** : AI can analyse historical data to forecast future market trends, helping

businesses make informed strategic decisions.

- **Example** : Use predictive analytics to forecast consumer demand for seasonal products, allowing businesses to adjust inventory levels accordingly.

Example Use Case: AI-Assisted Competitor Analysis

A small business might use AI-assisted market research to analyse its top three competitors. By scraping data from competitors' websites and social media accounts, AI can track changes in product offerings, pricing strategies, and customer sentiment. This data provides insights into how competitors are performing and helps the business adjust its strategies to gain a competitive edge.

Resources for AI-Assisted Market Research

- **Crimson Hexagon** : A social media analytics platform that uses AI to track and analyse consumer behaviour and brand sentiment across multiple channels.

- **BuzzSumo** : An AI tool that helps you track trending content and analyse what is working in your niche, offering insights into popular topics and key influencers.
- **Brandwatch** : A digital consumer intelligence platform that uses AI to monitor online conversations, offering insights into customer preferences and emerging market trends.
- **SurveyMonkey + GPT** : Automate survey creation and data analysis using AI tools like GPT integrated with platforms such as SurveyMonkey.
- **IBM Watson Analytics** : A powerful AI-driven tool for advanced data analysis, helping businesses uncover hidden patterns and trends in their market data.

Maximising Earnings from AI-Assisted Market Research

1. **Offer Custom Market Research Services** : Many businesses need market insights but lack the tools or expertise to gather and analyse data. Offer AI-powered market

research services, providing tailored reports and actionable recommendations.

2. **Develop Niche Expertise** : Specialising in a particular industry or market segment can make you more valuable to businesses within that niche. Develop deep expertise in areas like e-commerce, healthcare, or technology, and use AI to deliver specialised market research.

3. **Provide Competitor Analysis Packages** : Offer businesses regular competitor analysis reports using AI to track competitors' activities, product launches, and market performance.

4. **Sell Predictive Market Insights** : Use AI to forecast future market trends and offer this as a premium service to businesses looking to stay ahead of the competition. Predictive analytics can help businesses make proactive decisions about product development, marketing, and sales strategies.

5. **Create Data-Driven Content** : Produce AI-powered reports, white papers, or infographics based on market research, and sell these as premium content or use them to attract new clients. Market research insights are valuable assets for content marketing.

6. **Monetise Research Templates** : Develop AI-generated market research templates that businesses can purchase and customise. Offer templates for various industries or business objectives such as customer feedback, competitor analysis, or trend forecasting.

Additional Revenue Streams

1. **Affiliate Marketing for AI Tools** : Recommend AI market research tools like BuzzSumo, Brandwatch, or IBM Watson Analytics, and earn commissions through affiliate marketing. Many businesses need AI tools to conduct their own research.
2. **Market Research Consulting** : Offer consulting services to businesses that need help interpreting and applying market research data. Provide them with AI-driven insights and strategic recommendations.
3. **Offer Training and Workshops** : Create training programs or workshops to teach businesses how to use AI tools for market research. This could involve courses on AI-powered data analysis, web scraping, or sentiment analysis.

4. **Create AI-Driven Dashboards** : Build custom AI-powered dashboards that provide businesses with real-time insights into their market. These dashboards can be used to track competitor activity, customer sentiment, and emerging trends.
5. **Collaborate with Marketing Agencies** : Partner with digital marketing agencies to offer AI-powered market research services. These agencies often need market insights to guide their clients' marketing strategies, and your AI expertise can fill that gap.

Maximising Success with AI-Assisted Market Research

- **Keep Data Clean** : Ensure that the data collected is accurate and free from irrelevant or duplicated information. Use AI tools to filter and clean data before analysis.
- **Focus on Actionable Insights** : AI can generate vast amounts of data, but focus on delivering insights that businesses can act on. Summarise findings clearly and offer recommendations for strategy adjustments.
- **Stay Up-to-Date with AI Tools** : The field of AI-powered market research is rapidly

evolving. Stay informed about the latest tools and technologies to maintain a competitive edge.

- **Use A/B Testing** : Experiment with different research methods and data sources to see which delivers the most valuable insights. AI can help analyse these tests and refine your approach over time.
- **Integrate AI into Existing Platforms** : If you're working with clients who already use CRM or business intelligence tools, integrate AI research tools into their systems for seamless insights.

By conducting AI-assisted market research, you can offer businesses fast, accurate, and data-driven insights that improve decision-making. With multiple ways to monetise your services and an ever-growing demand for AI-powered research, this field offers significant earning potential.

Chapter 41
Writing and Selling Niche Articles

Writing and selling niche articles can be a highly profitable way to generate income, especially if you focus on specialised topics with dedicated audiences. By leveraging your expertise or using

AI tools like GPT, you can create high-quality content that appeals to specific market segments. This summary explores practical tips, examples, and resources to help you maximise your earning potential by writing and selling niche articles.

Importance of Writing Niche Articles

- **Higher Demand for Specialised Knowledge** : Niche topics often have fewer writers, which creates opportunities to provide valuable content that stands out.
- **Targeted Audiences** : Writing for a specific niche allows you to attract a dedicated readership or client base willing to pay for specialised knowledge.
- **Higher Earnings Potential** : Niche articles tend to command higher rates, as clients or readers are willing to pay more for expertise in less-common areas.
- **Authority and Credibility** : Consistently producing high-quality content in a niche helps you build credibility as an expert, leading to long-term clients and opportunities.

Practical Tips for Writing and Selling Niche Articles

1. **Identify a Profitable Niche** : Start by researching niche markets that are in demand but have relatively low competition. Popular niches include finance, health and wellness, technology, sustainability, and hobbies such as photography or gaming. Choose a niche where you either have knowledge or can quickly gain expertise.

   - **Example** : Writing articles on sustainable gardening practices may attract a loyal audience of eco-conscious readers.

2. **Research Audience Needs** : Understand the needs and pain points of your target audience. Research online forums, social media groups, and niche blogs to identify common questions or topics of interest.

   - **Example** : If writing for a health niche, investigate what common concerns people have about specific diets or wellness trends.

3. **Use AI for Content Research and Generation** : AI tools like GPT can assist in generating ideas, drafting content, or conducting research on niche topics. This allows you to write faster and focus on adding value through personal insights and expertise.

   - **Example** : Use GPT to generate an outline for an article on the latest trends in cryptocurrency or to suggest blog post ideas for a fitness website.

4. **Write Authoritative and Engaging Content** : Niche readers often seek in-depth knowledge and practical advice. Write content that is both informative and engaging, backed by reliable sources. Focus on delivering actionable tips, clear explanations, and real-life examples to keep your audience interested.

   - **Example** : For a finance niche, include specific investment strategies or examples of portfolio management to provide readers with practical takeaways.

5. **Create a Portfolio of Niche Articles** : Build a portfolio that showcases your best work in the niche you've chosen. Having a strong portfolio is crucial for attracting clients and demonstrating your expertise.

   - **Example** : If you're focusing on the travel niche, create a portfolio of articles on hidden travel destinations, budget travel tips, and unique experiences in various countries.

6. **Sell Articles on Content Platforms** : Platforms like Constant Content, iWriter, and Textbroker allow you to sell pre-written niche articles or take on custom writing jobs. These platforms are ideal for reaching clients who are specifically looking for niche content.

   - **Example** : Create a batch of articles on emerging technology trends and sell them on a content marketplace that specialises in tech content.

7. **Approach Niche Blogs and Websites** : Reach out to blogs, magazines, and websites in your chosen niche and offer to

write for them. Many niche websites are looking for freelance writers to provide content for their readers. Pitch article ideas that fit the style and audience of the publication.

- **Example** : A blog focused on plant-based diets may be interested in articles about the health benefits of veganism or recipes that support a plant-based lifestyle.

8. **Monetise Your Own Blog or Website** : Consider creating your own niche blog or website where you can publish your articles. Monetise through affiliate marketing, sponsored posts, or selling premium content like eBooks or paid guides.

- **Example** : Start a blog about DIY home projects and earn money by promoting home improvement tools through affiliate links or by selling an eBook on home renovation tips.

9. **Repurpose Content for Multiple Platforms** : Maximise your earning potential by repurposing your niche articles into different formats, such as video scripts,

podcasts, or social media posts. This allows you to reach a wider audience and create multiple revenue streams from the same content.

- **Example** : Turn a niche article on personal finance tips into a YouTube video series or a downloadable guide.

10. **Offer Ghostwriting Services** : Many businesses and individuals are willing to pay for ghostwritten content in niche areas. Offer ghostwriting services for clients who want to publish articles under their own name but need expert content.

- **Example** : Ghostwrite articles for a nutritionist or wellness coach on the benefits of certain diets, and charge premium rates for the expertise you provide.

Example Use Case: Writing Niche Articles on Cryptocurrency

Cryptocurrency is a growing niche with high demand for educational content, investment tips, and market analysis. You could write a series of articles explaining blockchain technology, offering insights into popular cryptocurrencies, or giving practical advice on how to invest in crypto. By selling these articles to crypto blogs or platforms, or publishing them on your own blog, you can tap into a lucrative market.

Resources for Writing and Selling Niche Articles

- **Content Platforms** : Constant Content, Textbroker, iWriter – these platforms allow you to sell pre-written articles or offer writing services to clients looking for niche content.
- **Freelance Marketplaces** : Upwork, Fiverr – ideal for finding clients who need niche-specific articles on a contract basis.
- **SEO Tools** : Ahrefs, SEMrush – use these tools to identify trending topics, keywords, and gaps in niche markets to write articles that rank highly on search engines.
- **Grammarly** : An essential tool to ensure your niche articles are polished and professional, with no grammar or spelling mistakes.
- **Google Trends** : Use Google Trends to discover trending topics and emerging

niches that could be profitable to write about.

Maximising Earnings from Writing and Selling Niche Articles

1. **Specialise in High-Paying Niches** : Certain niches, such as finance, healthcare, and technology, typically pay more due to the specialised knowledge required. Focus on these areas to maximise your rates.
2. **Offer Subscription-Based Services** : Provide ongoing content creation services for businesses that need regular articles in your niche. This could be on a weekly or monthly subscription basis, giving you recurring income.
3. **Create a Content Package** : Offer clients a content package that includes multiple articles, social media content, and blog posts. This increases the value of your services and allows you to charge a premium.
4. **Sell Exclusive Rights to Articles** : Selling exclusive rights to niche articles can earn you more than selling them as non-exclusive content. Clients who want unique content will pay a premium for exclusivity.

5. **Write for Print Magazines and Journals** : Many print publications in niche markets are willing to pay well for high-quality, expert content. Approach niche magazines and offer to write in-depth articles or features.
6. **Bundle Articles into E-Books** : Compile your niche articles into e-books or guides and sell them as a package. For example, you could write a series of health articles and turn them into an eBook on holistic wellness.

Additional Revenue Streams

1. **Affiliate Marketing** : Integrate affiliate links into your articles, especially if writing about products or services in your niche. You can earn commissions from sales generated through your links.
2. **Sell Courses or Workshops** : Create a course or workshop based on your niche expertise. For example, if you write about digital marketing, offer a course on content marketing strategies.
3. **Create a Paid Newsletter** : Offer a subscription-based newsletter that delivers premium niche articles and insights to your

audience. Newsletters are a great way to build a dedicated following and generate steady income.

4. **Offer Consulting Services** : As you establish yourself as an expert in your niche, you can offer consulting services to businesses or individuals who need advice or strategy development in that area.

Maximising Success with Niche Articles

- **Stay Current with Trends** : Keep up-to-date with the latest trends in your niche to ensure your articles remain relevant and in demand.
- **Focus on Quality** : Ensure your articles are well-researched and offer real value. Niche audiences are often highly knowledgeable, so providing accurate and in-depth content is key.
- **Network in Your Niche** : Build relationships with influencers, bloggers, and businesses within your niche. Networking can lead to guest blogging opportunities, collaborations, and more writing gigs.
- **Optimise for SEO** : Writing SEO-optimised content helps your articles rank higher on

search engines, increasing visibility and attracting more clients or readers.

By writing and selling niche articles, you can establish yourself as an expert, attract a dedicated readership, and unlock numerous income streams. Specialising in a profitable niche can significantly boost your earnings and create long-term business opportunities.

Chapter 42
Creating Personalised AI-Generated Letters

Personalised AI-generated letters are a growing niche, providing businesses and individuals with tailored communication solutions for various purposes. From business correspondence and client outreach to personal messages and invitations, AI tools such as GPT can streamline the letter-writing process, offering efficiency, customisation, and scalability. This summary explores practical tips, examples, and resources to help you maximise your earning potential by offering personalised AI-generated letter services.

Benefits of Creating Personalised AI-Generated Letters

- **Time Efficiency** : AI-powered tools can create high-quality letters quickly, saving time for businesses and individuals.
- **Customisation** : Personalisation options allow for specific tone, style, and content adjustments to meet individual client needs.
- **Scalability** : Whether it's creating one letter or hundreds, AI enables efficient mass customisation.
- **Cost-Effectiveness** : By automating the letter-writing process, you can offer competitive pricing for clients who need frequent or bulk letters.

Practical Tips for Creating Personalised AI-Generated Letters

1. **Understand Client Needs** : Start by getting a clear understanding of the type of letter your client requires, including tone (formal or casual), purpose (sales, customer support, personal message), and any specific details that need to be included.

- **Example** : A business may request a series of follow-up letters to clients, requiring a professional tone and key details such as the client's name and previous interaction history.

2. **Choose the Right AI Tool** : Tools like GPT can generate personalised letters, but selecting the right tool with proper customisation options is key. Some platforms allow more detailed personalisation, making the output feel more natural and relevant.

   - **Example** : Use GPT to create personalised thank-you letters after an event, ensuring each letter addresses the recipient by name and references specific details from the event.

3. **Create Templates for Common Letter Types** : Develop templates for frequently requested letters, such as cover letters, thank-you notes, invitation letters, and business proposals. These templates can be easily adjusted for each client, saving time and improving consistency.

- **Example** : Have a template for a customer service letter that can be adapted to various scenarios, such as handling complaints or providing follow-up information.

4. **Personalisation through Input Fields** : When offering AI-generated letters, set up custom input fields to gather necessary personal details from clients, such as names, company information, and any specific requests. This information will be used to generate highly personalised and accurate letters.

   - **Example** : If creating wedding invitation letters, input details like the couple's names, venue, and date to ensure the letter is unique to each client.

5. **Adjust Tone and Style to Fit the Occasion** : Use AI to fine-tune the tone and style of the letter according to the client's needs. Whether they require a formal business letter or a warm, personalised note, ensure the AI-generated content reflects the appropriate mood.

- **Example** : For a business partnership proposal letter, maintain a professional and persuasive tone, while for personal thank-you letters, focus on a heartfelt and appreciative style.

6. **Proofread and Edit for Accuracy** : While AI-generated content can be high quality, it's important to review each letter for accuracy, personalisation, and tone. Ensure the content is free of errors and that the AI has included all the necessary details requested by the client.

   - **Example** : For a job application cover letter, review the generated content to ensure it addresses the right company, position, and qualifications in a persuasive manner.

7. **Offer Bulk Personalisation for Businesses** : Many businesses need to send personalised letters in bulk, such as customer outreach emails, holiday greetings, or follow-up communications. By automating this process with AI, you can offer a scalable solution that saves clients time while maintaining a personal touch.

- **Example** : Provide a bulk letter service for a company looking to send personalised holiday greetings to hundreds of clients, using an AI template that customises each letter with client names and specific details.

8. **Provide a Variety of Letter Types** : Expand your offerings by providing different types of letters for various purposes—personal letters, business letters, invitation letters, and even emotional or congratulatory letters.

- **Example** : Offer services to write condolence letters, congratulations messages, or holiday invitations, depending on the client's needs.

9. **Monetise Customisation Options** : Offer additional customisation for a premium price, such as including specific formatting, adding graphics or logos, or using a specific writing style. These options can make your service more appealing to clients looking for extra value.

- **Example** : Charge extra for custom logos or specific branding in business letters, or offer handwritten fonts for personal notes to give a more personal touch.

Resources for Personalised AI-Generated Letters

- **AI Writing Tools** : Use platforms like OpenAI's GPT, Copy.ai, or Jasper to generate personalised letters quickly and accurately.
- **Freelance Marketplaces** : Fiverr, Upwork – offer your personalised letter-writing services to clients looking for custom letters, whether for business or personal purposes.
- **CRM Software** : Integrate AI-generated letters with Customer Relationship Management (CRM) software to help businesses send personalised letters as part of their customer outreach strategy.
- **Grammarly** : Use this tool to ensure that AI-generated letters are grammatically correct and professional.
- **Mail Merge Tools** : Consider using mail merge tools for sending out bulk personalised letters via email, particularly for

businesses needing efficient mass communication.

Examples of Personalised AI-Generated Letters

1. **Business Proposal Letter** : Tailor each proposal letter to a different client or potential partner, ensuring that the content addresses their specific needs and includes relevant data.

    - **Example** : A marketing agency can use AI to generate business proposal letters that showcase their services in a personalised way for each prospect.

2. **Thank-You Letters** : Use AI to create heartfelt thank-you notes after events, business transactions, or personal milestones. Personalising these letters can leave a lasting impression on recipients.

    - **Example** : A charity might use AI to send personalised thank-you letters to each donor, referencing their specific donation and how it made an impact.

3. **Customer Service Letters** : Automate the generation of customer service responses to provide quick, personalised solutions to customer inquiries or complaints. The use of AI can maintain professionalism while addressing specific customer issues.

   - **Example** : A company can automate its responses to common customer service queries, saving time while ensuring a personalised reply.

Maximising Your Earnings with AI-Generated Letters

1. **Offer Subscription Services** : Provide a subscription service for businesses or individuals who need regular, personalised letters, such as monthly client outreach or holiday messages.
2. **Bundle Services** : Package letter writing with other services, such as resume writing or content creation, to increase the overall value of your offerings.
3. **Offer Corporate Packages** : Target businesses that need large-scale personalised communication, such as

marketing agencies or event planners, and offer packages for bulk personalised letters.

4. **Add Additional Fees for High-Level Personalisation** : Charge higher fees for clients who require extra personalisation or advanced features, such as unique branding, advanced formatting, or personalised follow-up sequences.

Success Factors for Creating Personalised AI-Generated Letters

- **High-Quality Personalisation** : Ensure that the letters are truly tailored to the client's needs, offering a high level of personalisation in terms of tone, content, and format.
- **Speed and Efficiency** : Leverage AI to provide quick turnaround times for clients needing immediate communication solutions.
- **Competitive Pricing** : By automating much of the letter-writing process, you can offer competitive prices while maintaining high standards of quality.
- **Offer a Range of Letter Types** : The more types of personalised letters you offer, the more diverse your client base will be, from

businesses needing formal correspondence to individuals seeking personal messages.

Creating personalised AI-generated letters is a growing business opportunity that leverages AI's ability to efficiently craft tailored messages. By offering a wide range of letter types and ensuring high-quality personalisation, you can establish a profitable service that appeals to both businesses and individuals.

Chapter 43
Offering AI Content Auditing Services

AI content auditing services offer businesses a streamlined way to evaluate, optimise, and improve their content. Whether it's for SEO, readability, brand consistency, or overall quality, AI tools can audit large volumes of content quickly and efficiently. This summary explores how you can offer AI-powered content auditing services and includes practical tips, examples, and resources to maximise your earning potential in this niche.

Benefits of Offering AI Content Auditing Services

- **Efficiency** : AI tools can scan and audit vast amounts of content in a fraction of the time it would take manually.
- **Consistency** : Ensures that all content meets quality, tone, and brand guidelines across various platforms.
- **Actionable Insights** : AI identifies areas for improvement, providing data-driven suggestions for content enhancement.
- **Scalability** : Easily handle large projects, offering services to both small businesses and large enterprises.

Practical Tips for Offering AI Content Auditing Services

1. **Define the Scope of Your Service**
   Decide what types of content you will audit and the key metrics to focus on. This could include SEO optimisation, tone of voice, grammatical accuracy, brand consistency, or content structure.

- **Example** : Offer SEO-focused audits where AI checks keyword density, metadata, and link structure to improve rankings.

2. **Use Reliable AI Tools**
   There are various AI tools available for content auditing. Choose the right ones based on the service you're offering.

   - **Example** : Tools like MarketMuse and Clearscope are ideal for SEO audits, while Grammarly or Hemingway Editor can evaluate grammar and readability.

3. **Offer a Comprehensive Report**
   Provide clients with a detailed report that outlines the strengths and weaknesses of their content. Include actionable insights and recommendations for improvement.

   - **Example** : After an audit, provide a report showing how the client's blog posts can be optimised for readability and SEO, alongside specific steps to improve performance.

4. **Evaluate SEO Metrics**
   AI tools can analyse content for SEO
   efficiency. Offer services where you audit
   metadata, keyword placement, internal
   linking, and overall search visibility.

   - **Example** : Use an AI tool like
     SurferSEO to audit and improve blog
     posts or website pages to better align
     with target keywords and increase
     search engine rankings.

5. **Customise Audits for Brand Consistency**
   Ensure the content aligns with the client's
   brand voice and guidelines. AI tools can
   assess tone and consistency across multiple
   pieces of content.

   - **Example** : Offer services where you
     ensure that product descriptions,
     website pages, and social media posts
     all reflect a consistent brand tone and
     style.

6. **Run Readability and Accessibility
   Checks**
   AI can help ensure that content is readable
   and accessible to diverse audiences,

providing value to businesses that aim for inclusivity.

- **Example** : Use tools like Hemingway to measure readability, ensuring that a client's content is easy to understand for a wide audience, or AI-powered accessibility checkers to ensure compliance with digital accessibility standards.

7. **Offer Competitive Pricing Based on Volume**
Offer different pricing tiers depending on the amount of content to be audited. For example, provide bulk audits for large businesses and smaller packages for startups or individuals.

- **Example** : Create a pricing plan that scales depending on how many pages or articles need auditing, offering discounts for larger projects.

8. **Automate Re-auditing for Ongoing Improvement**
Offer subscription services for clients who want regular audits of their content. This

helps businesses stay on top of content quality over time.

- **Example** : Provide quarterly audits to clients, ensuring their content stays optimised as search algorithms or brand guidelines evolve.

9. **Audit for Plagiarism and Originality**
Ensure the originality of content by using AI tools to detect plagiarism. This is crucial for businesses that publish a high volume of content.

- **Example** : Use tools like Copyscape or Turnitin to audit content for originality and offer recommendations to make content more unique.

10. **Collaborate with Content Creators**
Partner with copywriters, marketers, or SEO professionals to provide end-to-end content services, from auditing to content creation and optimisation.
- **Example** : Offer a service where you audit existing content and then collaborate with writers to make necessary improvements or create new optimised content based on audit results.

Resources for AI Content Auditing Services

- **Grammarly** : A tool that evaluates grammar, spelling, and tone to ensure high-quality content.
- **MarketMuse** : An AI platform for content research, planning, and optimisation, focused on improving SEO.
- **SurferSEO** : A tool that analyses keyword usage and search engine optimisation to ensure better rankings.
- **Clearscope** : A content optimisation tool that improves the relevance and SEO of written content.
- **Copyscape** : A plagiarism detection tool to ensure content originality.

Examples of AI Content Auditing in Action

1. **SEO Blog Audit**
   A client requests an audit of their blog for SEO optimisation. You use AI tools to assess keyword density, readability, and metadata. The audit reveals areas where keywords are underutilised and suggests improvements for title tags and internal linking structures.

2. **E-commerce Product Description Audit**
   An e-commerce business asks for a brand consistency audit across its product descriptions. You run AI tools to ensure that all descriptions maintain a consistent tone, style, and SEO alignment, helping the client improve both their brand image and search rankings.
3. **Readability Audit for Marketing Emails**
   A company's email marketing strategy needs improvement. You use AI to audit the readability of their marketing emails, ensuring they're clear and engaging. The audit suggests simplifying sentence structure and using more customer-centric language.

Maximising Your Earnings with AI Content Auditing

1. **Offer Different Service Packages** : Provide tiered services, such as basic audits (SEO and grammar) and advanced audits (brand consistency, accessibility, and plagiarism checks).
2. **Subscription-Based Services** : Provide ongoing audits as content is updated or new

content is added, ensuring continuous optimisation.

3. **Add-On Services** : Upsell content optimisation or rewriting services alongside the audit, allowing clients to immediately implement your recommendations.
4. **Collaborate with Agencies** : Partner with marketing or content agencies that may require regular auditing services for their clients.

Success Factors for AI Content Auditing

- **Accuracy and Detail** : Clients expect precise, actionable insights. Use a combination of AI tools and manual checking to provide thorough audits.
- **Efficiency** : Provide fast turnaround times, taking advantage of AI's speed to deliver results quickly without sacrificing quality.
- **Scalable Solutions** : Offer services that can handle large content volumes, making your service attractive to businesses with significant content needs.

Offering AI-powered content auditing services is an excellent way to help businesses enhance their content performance, improve SEO, and maintain brand consistency. By leveraging the latest AI tools and providing comprehensive, scalable solutions, you can create a profitable niche with recurring revenue potential.

Chapter 44
Developing AI-Generated Quizzes and Games

AI-generated quizzes and games are rapidly becoming popular tools for engagement, education, and entertainment across various industries. By leveraging AI, you can create interactive and personalised content that resonates with users, whether for educational platforms, marketing campaigns, or entertainment applications. This summary explores how to develop AI-generated quizzes and games, offering practical tips, examples, and resources to help you maximise your earning potential in this niche.

Benefits of AI-Generated Quizzes and Games

- **Engagement** : Interactive content such as quizzes and games increases user engagement and retention.

- **Personalisation** : AI can adapt content based on user responses, creating a personalised experience.
- **Scalability** : AI allows for the rapid creation of multiple quizzes or games tailored to different audiences.
- **Efficiency** : AI can generate content faster and more efficiently than manual creation, saving time and resources.

Practical Tips for Developing AI-Generated Quizzes and Games

1. **Choose Your Niche**
   Decide whether your focus will be educational, entertainment, or marketing quizzes and games. Each niche has unique needs and audiences.

   - **Example** : In the educational space, develop quizzes that test knowledge and reinforce learning, while in marketing, focus on fun quizzes that drive user engagement and brand awareness.

2. **Utilise AI Tools for Quiz Generation**
   Use AI platforms like Quizizz, Riddle, or Typeform for quiz creation, as these tools offer AI-powered functionalities to help generate questions, answers, and scoring.

   - **Example** : AI can automatically suggest multiple-choice questions based on a specific subject or topic, reducing the workload of manual question creation.

3. **Implement Personalised Experiences**
   AI enables personalised quiz and game experiences by adapting questions or challenges based on user input. This enhances engagement and creates a more meaningful user journey.

   - **Example** : If a user answers a question incorrectly, AI can generate simpler follow-up questions to reinforce learning or adjust the difficulty level based on performance.

4. **Integrate Gamification Elements**
   Incorporate game mechanics such as scoring, rewards, and leaderboards to

enhance the interactive aspect of your quizzes and games. This increases user retention and encourages repeated participation.

- **Example** : Use AI to generate dynamic leaderboards that show real-time results, or offer rewards such as badges or points for completing quiz levels.

5. **Create Educational Quizzes for Schools and Businesses**
AI-generated quizzes are ideal for educational platforms, corporate training, or employee assessments. Customise quizzes for specific subjects, courses, or industries, and provide detailed feedback through AI.

- **Example** : Develop quizzes for a corporate client's training programme, where AI analyses employee performance and suggests areas for improvement.

6. **Monetise Your Quizzes and Games**
Offer your services to businesses, schools, or entertainment platforms. You can also

sell your AI-generated quizzes as products or subscription-based services.

- **Example** : Create and sell quiz packages to educators or e-learning platforms, or offer subscription services where businesses receive customised, regularly updated quizzes for employee training.

7. **Use AI to Analyse User Behaviour**
AI tools can track user responses and behaviour, allowing for deeper insights into how users engage with quizzes or games. This data can be used to improve future content or demonstrate value to clients.

- **Example** : Offer analytics services to clients where you track quiz completion rates, average scores, and user engagement metrics, providing valuable insights for marketing campaigns or educational improvements.

8. **Generate Adaptive Learning Games**
Create AI-powered games that adapt to user performance in real-time, making learning more interactive and fun. These games can

automatically adjust difficulty based on how well users perform.

- **Example** : Develop an educational game where the difficulty increases as the user answers questions correctly, keeping them engaged and motivated to continue learning.

9. **Offer Customisation for Businesses**
Businesses may seek customised quizzes or games tailored to their brand or goals. Offer services where you generate quizzes or games with branded themes, questions related to the company's products, or gamified marketing strategies.

- **Example** : For a retail client, develop a branded quiz that helps users find the perfect product based on their answers, incorporating AI to personalise the recommendations.

10. **Collaborate with App Developers**
Work with app developers to integrate AI-generated quizzes and games into mobile apps. This opens up opportunities for subscription models or in-app purchases.

- **Example** : Collaborate with an educational app developer to integrate quizzes that adapt to users' learning levels, providing ongoing engagement and upsell opportunities for advanced learning modules.

Resources for Developing AI-Generated Quizzes and Games

- **Quizizz** : A platform for creating engaging quizzes for both education and entertainment purposes.
- **Typeform** : An interactive form and quiz creation tool that allows for personalisation and data analysis.
- **Kahoot!** : A game-based learning platform that enables the creation of interactive quizzes for education or entertainment.
- **Playbuzz** : A tool for creating viral quizzes and games, often used in marketing to engage users.

Examples of AI-Generated Quizzes and Games in Action

1. **Corporate Training Quizzes**
   A company seeks to improve employee training. You use AI to generate custom quizzes that assess employee knowledge on specific company policies. The AI tracks results and generates reports that help the company identify knowledge gaps and focus future training efforts.
2. **E-Learning Platforms**
   You create adaptive learning quizzes for an e-learning platform. AI adjusts the difficulty of questions based on the user's performance, offering a personalised learning experience that helps users progress at their own pace.
3. **Entertainment Quizzes for Social Media**
   A brand wants to engage users through social media. You develop fun, viral quizzes using AI, which adapts questions based on user preferences and provides personalised results that align with the brand's products or services.

Maximising Your Earnings with AI-Generated Quizzes and Games

1. **Offer Customisation Services** : Provide businesses or educators with tailored quizzes or games that align with their specific needs, whether for training, marketing, or education.
2. **Create Subscription-Based Models** : Offer ongoing quiz or game generation services where clients receive fresh content regularly.
3. **Partner with E-Learning Platforms** : Collaborate with e-learning platforms to provide ongoing quiz content that enhances user engagement and retention.
4. **Licensing Opportunities** : License your quizzes and games to other businesses, allowing them to use the content while you retain ownership and rights.

Success Factors for AI-Generated Quizzes and Games

- **User Engagement** : Ensure the quizzes and games are interactive, engaging, and aligned with the target audience's interests.

- **Personalisation** : Use AI to provide personalised experiences, adjusting content based on user responses and preferences.
- **Quality Content** : Ensure that the questions, challenges, and scenarios are well-thought-out and relevant to the goals of the quiz or game.
- **Analytics and Feedback** : Use AI tools to provide detailed analytics on user performance and engagement, giving your clients valuable insights to improve their content strategy.

Developing AI-generated quizzes and games offers a versatile, scalable way to create engaging content for various industries. By leveraging AI's speed, personalisation capabilities, and ability to generate detailed insights, you can build a profitable business that meets the growing demand for interactive, tailored experiences.

Chapter 45
Assisting with Grant and Proposal Writing

AI-assisted grant and proposal writing is a growing field where technology can significantly streamline the process of creating compelling, detailed, and persuasive proposals. By leveraging AI, writers can quickly generate, optimise, and refine grant applications, proposals, and funding requests for a variety of sectors. This summary provides practical tips, examples, and resources to help you maximise your earning potential by offering AI-powered grant and proposal writing services.

Benefits of AI in Grant and Proposal Writing

- **Efficiency** : AI tools can automate large portions of the writing process, allowing you to draft complex proposals more quickly.
- **Consistency** : AI ensures that proposals maintain a consistent tone, style, and structure across different sections.
- **Accuracy** : With AI, you can better manage formatting, citations, and compliance with specific grant or funding guidelines.
- **Data-Driven** : AI can analyse past successful proposals and provide insights into best practices, increasing the likelihood of success.

Practical Tips for Assisting with Grant and Proposal Writing

1. **Understand the Client's Needs and Goals**
   Each grant or proposal will have unique requirements. Familiarise yourself with the client's goals and the specifics of the funding opportunity to tailor your writing accordingly.

   - **Example** : A charity seeking funding for community projects will have different goals from a business applying for research and development grants. Tailor the proposal content to address the funder's specific interests.

2. **Use AI Tools to Draft Proposals**
   AI writing assistants like GPT, Wordtune, and Grammarly can help generate sections of proposals, such as introductions, project overviews, and budget justifications. These tools save time by automating repetitive writing tasks while ensuring clarity and coherence.

   - **Example** : Use GPT to draft a compelling project summary, then refine it with specific details relevant to the client's objectives.

3. **Follow Grant Guidelines Closely**
   AI tools can help ensure that proposals follow strict formatting and submission guidelines, a crucial factor in grant writing. Use these tools to double-check adherence to word limits, citation formats, and structural requirements.

   - **Example** : After drafting a grant application, use AI to confirm that the proposal complies with page length, font size, and specific submission rules laid out by the funder.

4. **Incorporate Strong Data and Evidence**
   AI can assist in researching and integrating relevant data into the proposal, such as statistics, previous research, and case studies that strengthen your arguments. This makes your proposal more compelling and evidence-based.

   - **Example** : Use AI-powered research tools to gather supporting data on the impact of the project you're proposing and integrate that data seamlessly into the narrative.

5. **Optimise for Readability and Clarity**
   AI writing tools can review your drafts for clarity, tone, and readability, ensuring that complex ideas are communicated effectively. This is especially important when addressing technical or highly specialised topics in grant proposals.

   - **Example** : Grammarly or Hemingway Editor can help ensure that your writing is clear, free from jargon, and accessible to a non-specialist audience, which is often essential for grants.

6. **Develop a Persuasive Executive Summary**
   The executive summary is one of the most critical parts of a grant proposal. Use AI tools to craft a concise and persuasive summary that outlines the project's goals, methods, and expected outcomes, highlighting its importance.

   - **Example** : An AI-powered content generator can help create a draft executive summary, which you can then customise to reflect the unique aspects of the client's project.

7. **Create Detailed Budgets and Timelines**
   AI can assist with creating detailed project budgets and timelines, helping to break down costs and time allocations in a way that aligns with the grant's requirements.

   - **Example** : Tools like Excel paired with AI can generate accurate budget forecasts, ensuring that all project expenses are accounted for, from staffing to materials.

8. **Review and Edit Collaboratively**
   AI writing tools allow for real-time collaborative editing, making it easy to refine the proposal with input from the client or team members. This ensures the final document is polished and reflects the collective input.

   - **Example** : Use Google Docs with integrated AI tools for seamless collaboration, allowing multiple stakeholders to comment and make edits simultaneously.

9. **Tailor Proposals to Specific Funders**
   Use AI to customise proposals for different funders, ensuring that each submission aligns with their priorities, goals, and funding criteria. This increases the chances of success by demonstrating that you understand the funder's mission.

   - **Example** : AI can quickly modify a proposal by adjusting key phrases and objectives to align with different funders' interests, such as sustainability, community development, or innovation.

10. **Offer Multiple Drafts and Revisions**
    AI tools can speed up the revision process, allowing you to provide clients with multiple drafts of a proposal in a shorter time. Offering revision services will make your grant writing package more attractive to clients.
- **Example** : Generate a rough first draft using AI, then refine the language and structure in later drafts, incorporating client feedback at each stage.

Resources for AI-Enhanced Grant and Proposal Writing

- **Grammarly** : An AI-powered writing assistant that improves clarity, grammar, and style, essential for high-quality proposals.
- **WriteSonic** : A content generation tool that can help create sections of grant proposals quickly.
- **Wordtune** : A tool that provides AI-driven suggestions for improving tone and readability, perfect for ensuring persuasive and accessible proposals.
- **Google Scholar** : An AI-powered research tool that helps gather relevant academic papers and data to support your grant proposals.

Examples of AI-Assisted Grant Writing in Action

1. **Non-Profit Grant Proposal**
   A non-profit organisation seeks funding for an environmental conservation project. You use AI to draft a detailed project description, budget forecast, and timeline, ensuring that the proposal follows the specific

requirements of the funder. The AI tool also helps optimise the executive summary for maximum impact.

2. **Research Funding Application**
   A university researcher applies for a scientific grant to support a new study. You use AI to generate a literature review, ensuring the proposal includes the latest research in the field. AI also helps structure the project methodology, ensuring clarity and precision.

3. **Business Development Proposal**
   A small business applies for a government grant to support its expansion into green energy solutions. Using AI, you draft a persuasive argument for why the business should receive funding, supported by relevant market research and financial projections.

Maximising Your Earnings with AI-Enhanced Grant Writing

1. **Offer Proposal Packages** : Provide clients with different packages, from basic drafting services to comprehensive grant-writing and editing services.

2. **Specialise in High-Demand Sectors** : Focus on industries with consistent funding needs, such as education, healthcare, or environmental projects, to attract more clients.
3. **Create a Subscription Model** : Offer ongoing support to clients applying for multiple grants over time, providing value through continuous service and increasing recurring income.
4. **Upsell Editing and Review Services** : Include additional services such as grant reviews, compliance checks, and proofreading to maximise revenue.

Success Factors for Grant and Proposal Writing

- **Attention to Detail** : Ensure that every proposal follows the funder's guidelines and addresses their priorities clearly and accurately.
- **Persuasive Narrative** : Create a compelling, data-driven narrative that clearly communicates the need for funding and the potential impact of the project.
- **Clear, Concise Writing** : Proposals should be easy to read and free of jargon, making it

simple for reviewers to understand the project's value.

- **Timely Submission** : Ensure that all proposals are completed and submitted on time, as deadlines are critical in grant writing.

By offering AI-enhanced grant and proposal writing services, you can help clients secure vital funding for their projects while building a profitable business for yourself. The combination of efficiency, customisation, and scalability provided by AI tools allows you to deliver high-quality proposals at a faster rate, maximising both client satisfaction and your earning potential.

Chapter 46
Personalised Gift Ideas Using GPT

Leveraging AI, particularly GPT-powered tools, can help generate unique and creative personalised gift ideas for clients or businesses looking to offer tailored gifting services. AI can quickly analyse preferences, interests, and occasions to recommend thoughtful, customised gifts. This summary outlines practical tips, examples, and resources to help you maximise your earning potential by offering personalised gift ideas using GPT.

Benefits of GPT for Personalised Gift Ideas

- **Customisation** : GPT can quickly generate gift suggestions tailored to individual tastes and preferences based on limited input, making the process of finding the perfect gift faster and more accurate.
- **Efficiency** : By automating the brainstorming process, AI saves time when coming up with gift ideas, particularly for niche or hard-to-shop-for individuals.
- **Scalability** : For businesses offering gifting services, GPT allows you to scale your personalised gift recommendations for multiple clients without sacrificing quality.

Practical Tips for Offering Personalised Gift Ideas Using GPT

1. **Gather Key Information**
   The more detailed the input, the better the output. Collect information about the recipient's hobbies, favourite brands, interests, and the occasion for gifting.

- **Example** : If a customer says the recipient loves reading, cooking, and sustainable products, GPT can generate gift ideas like eco-friendly recipe books or sustainable kitchen gadgets.

2. **Utilise GPT for Niche Gift Suggestions**
GPT excels at generating personalised ideas for niche interests. For example, if someone is a fan of a particular film genre or historical period, GPT can suggest relevant, themed gifts.

   - **Example** : For someone who loves classic cinema, GPT could suggest vintage movie posters, memorabilia, or rare editions of famous scripts.

3. **Personalise with Custom Messages**
In addition to recommending gifts, GPT can help write personalised gift messages or notes to accompany the gift, making the experience even more special.

   - **Example** : Use GPT to craft a heartfelt message or poem based on the recipient's interests and the relationship with the gift giver.

4. **Create Gift Baskets or Bundles**
   GPT can generate ideas for curated gift baskets or bundles that align with the recipient's preferences.

   - **Example** : For a wellness enthusiast, GPT could recommend a gift basket filled with organic teas, essential oils, and mindfulness journals.

5. **Use AI to Offer Last-Minute Gift Ideas**
   For those seeking last-minute gifts, GPT can quickly suggest digital gift options such as e-books, online courses, or subscriptions tailored to the recipient's interests.

   - **Example** : If someone is interested in photography, GPT can recommend an online photography course or a premium subscription to a photography magazine.

6. **Upsell Personalised Gift Wrapping and Packaging**
   Offer additional services such as custom gift

wrapping and packaging suggestions. GPT can generate ideas for creative ways to package gifts, especially for special occasions.

- **Example** : Suggest eco-friendly wrapping options like reusable cloth wraps or customisable boxes with personalised messages printed on them.

7. **Build a Gifting Subscription Service**
Use GPT to power a gifting subscription service where clients can receive personalised gift ideas for every special occasion throughout the year, based on the recipient's evolving preferences.

- **Example** : A monthly subscription where clients provide updated details, and GPT generates new gift ideas for each birthday, anniversary, or holiday.

Examples of Personalised Gift Ideas Using GPT

1. **For the Tech Enthusiast**
GPT might recommend gadgets like

wireless chargers, smart home devices, or personalised phone cases. Adding a custom element, like engraved initials or a special message, elevates the gift.

2. **For the Foodie**
   Gift suggestions might include gourmet food baskets, a personalised cutting board, or a cooking class with a local chef. GPT can even suggest pairings like fine wines with cheeses or artisanal snacks.

3. **For the Traveller**
   AI could generate ideas like a personalised map of places they've visited, custom luggage tags, or travel-themed subscriptions such as monthly boxes filled with snacks from around the world.

4. **For the Fitness Buff**
   GPT could suggest personalised workout gear, smart fitness devices, or a subscription to a fitness app. Adding a personal touch, such as monogrammed towels or a custom yoga mat, makes the gift even more unique.

5. **For the Book Lover**
   In this case, GPT might recommend personalised bookplates, a curated collection of limited-edition books, or a subscription to a literary service that delivers handpicked books based on the recipient's favourite genres.

1. **Offer Gifting Services for Special Occasions**
   Cater to holidays, birthdays, and special events by offering a service that provides personalised gift suggestions year-round. GPT can help keep ideas fresh and tailored to each client's specific needs.

2. **Partner with E-commerce Platforms**
   Collaborate with online stores to offer a personalised gift service where users input preferences, and GPT generates tailored suggestions directly linked to purchasable products on the platform.

3. **Create a Personalised Gift Concierge Service**
   Offer a premium service that uses GPT to not only recommend gifts but also handle the purchase, packaging, and delivery of gifts on behalf of clients.

4. **Launch a Customised Gift Shop**
   Build a digital gift shop powered by GPT, where users can input the recipient's interests and receive curated gift suggestions that they can purchase directly from your site.

Resources for Personalised Gift Ideas Using GPT

- **Giftastic** : A tool that helps generate personalised gift ideas based on user input.
- **GPT-3-based apps** : Tools like Copy.ai or Jasper can be used to generate creative gift ideas quickly and efficiently.
- **AI-Powered E-commerce Integration** : Platforms like Shopify have plugins that integrate AI for personalised product recommendations, making it easier to offer a seamless shopping experience.

Success Factors for Personalised Gift Ideas

- **Attention to Detail** : The more specific the input, the more accurate and personalised the gift recommendations will be.
- **Timeliness** : Ensure that the service is efficient, especially for last-minute shoppers.
- **Creativity** : Offer unique and out-of-the-box gift ideas to set your service apart from generic gift suggestion platforms.

By using GPT to offer personalised gift ideas, you can help clients find the perfect present while building a profitable and scalable business. AI not only saves time but also allows you to offer highly customised services that can be tailored to various occasions, interests, and preferences, ultimately maximising both client satisfaction and your earnings potential.

Chapter 47
AI-Powered Coding and Debugging Assistance

The advent of AI-powered tools, particularly those driven by advanced models like GPT, has revolutionised coding and debugging. These tools offer developers and businesses powerful assistance to streamline development processes, reduce errors, and enhance productivity. This summary outlines practical tips, examples, and resources to help you maximise your earning potential by leveraging AI for coding and debugging tasks.

Benefits of AI in Coding and Debugging

1. **Faster Coding** : AI can assist with generating code snippets, automating

repetitive tasks, and offering solutions based on best practices.

2. **Enhanced Debugging** : AI tools help identify errors in code quickly, recommend fixes, and ensure higher code quality.

3. **Increased Productivity** : By automating mundane tasks, developers can focus on complex problems, improving efficiency and reducing development timelines.

4. **Accessibility for Non-Experts** : AI-powered coding assistance enables those with limited programming experience to write functional code, lowering barriers to entry.

Practical Tips for Maximising AI Coding and Debugging Assistance

1. **Use AI for Code Autocompletion** Many AI tools can predict and complete lines of code based on context, which speeds up the development process. Leverage these tools when writing large blocks of code or working on repetitive tasks.

   - **Example** : Tools like GitHub Copilot can predict and suggest lines of code as you write, reducing the need for

manual typing and speeding up
coding.

2. **AI-Assisted Debugging** Debugging often
   involves tracing errors in complex code. AI
   tools can detect bugs, highlight problematic
   code sections, and suggest corrections. This
   can save significant time during
   development.

   - **Example** : AI debugging tools like
     DeepCode scan your code for potential
     errors, inefficiencies, or security
     vulnerabilities, offering instant
     feedback for improvements.

3. **Learn from AI-Generated Solutions** Use
   AI-generated code as a learning tool. When
   AI suggests solutions, study the code to
   understand its logic, making you a better
   programmer in the long run.

   - **Example** : If GPT suggests an optimal
     algorithm for solving a problem, review
     the logic and apply it to similar
     problems in the future.

4. **Automate Repetitive Coding Tasks** AI can handle mundane tasks like generating boilerplate code, documentation, or setting up environments, freeing up time for more strategic work.

   - **Example** : AI-powered tools can automate the creation of setup scripts, configuration files, or unit tests, which often consume valuable time.

5. **Utilise AI for Refactoring** Refactoring code to improve readability and performance is time-consuming. AI can assist in recommending refactoring strategies that maintain code functionality while optimising efficiency.

   - **Example** : AI tools like Sourcery suggest better ways to write your code, reducing complexity while maintaining performance.

6. **Collaborate with AI in Pair Programming** Pair programming with AI can enhance collaboration by providing real-time suggestions, code reviews, and error detection.

- **Example** : With tools like GitHub Copilot, you can 'pair program' with the AI, which will assist you with ideas, best practices, and alternatives as you code.

7. **Use AI for Language Translations and Framework Adaptations** AI tools can help translate code from one programming language to another or suggest ways to adapt a solution from one framework to another.

- **Example** : GPT can assist in translating Python code into Java or suggest how to adapt a React component into a Vue.js component.

Examples of AI-Powered Coding and Debugging Assistance

1. **Code Snippet Generation** AI can quickly generate frequently used code snippets, such as login forms, database queries, or API integration.

- **Example** : GPT can generate code for a user authentication system or a RESTful API connection in Python, JavaScript, or any other programming language.

2. **Automated Testing** AI can assist in generating unit tests, integration tests, and even identify test cases that might have been missed during manual coding.

  - **Example** : Use GPT to generate test cases for each function or method in your codebase, ensuring comprehensive test coverage.

3. **Real-Time Error Fixing** AI tools can detect syntax errors, logical errors, or security vulnerabilities in real time, suggesting corrections as you write the code.

  - **Example** : AI-powered IDE extensions like TabNine provide error-checking and suggest fixes based on the specific context of your code.

4. **AI-Assisted Code Reviews** AI tools can review your code for best practices, security vulnerabilities, or optimisation opportunities, automating a traditionally manual process.

   - **Example** : Automated code review tools like Codacy analyse your code for issues such as complexity, duplication, and security risks, offering suggestions for improvement.

5. **Code Optimisation** AI can identify inefficient code and suggest optimisations to improve performance.

   - **Example** : GPT can suggest ways to optimise a for-loop, reduce database query load, or streamline API calls, resulting in faster and more efficient code execution.

Maximising Earnings with AI Coding and Debugging

1. **Offer AI-Enhanced Coding Services** Provide coding services where you use AI to generate fast, reliable code solutions for

clients. Market your efficiency and AI expertise as a competitive advantage.

- **Example** : Offer a service that quickly generates website components, API integrations, or backend logic using AI tools.

2. **AI-Powered Debugging as a Service**
   Market yourself as an expert in AI-assisted debugging. Use AI to quickly identify and fix issues in legacy systems or large codebases, offering faster solutions than traditional debugging methods.

   - **Example** : Provide a service that scans clients' codebases, identifies bugs, and optimises performance using AI tools like DeepCode.

3. **Develop AI Tools for Coding Communities** Create AI-powered tools for specific coding languages or frameworks. By offering a niche solution, you can sell or license the tool to developers and companies.

- **Example** : Build an AI plugin that helps React developers automatically generate components based on design inputs.

4. **Automate and Streamline Code Review Processes** Set up AI-powered code review services for development teams, offering automated reviews for code quality, security, and performance.

    - **Example** : Offer subscription-based code review services using AI to analyse code for potential bugs and performance issues.

5. **AI-Powered Code Refactoring** Provide a service that focuses on refactoring legacy code using AI tools to improve performance, scalability, and readability.

    - **Example** : Market yourself as a specialist who can take old or inefficient codebases and modernise them using AI-driven refactoring techniques.

Resources for AI Coding and Debugging

- **GitHub Copilot** : Offers AI-powered code suggestions and autocompletion.
- **TabNine** : An AI assistant for code completion, supporting multiple languages and frameworks.
- **DeepCode** : An AI tool that analyses code for bugs and vulnerabilities.
- **Sourcery** : AI-powered code refactoring tool that suggests improvements for your code.

Success Factors in AI Coding and Debugging

1. **Accuracy** : The quality of AI-generated code depends on the quality of the input. Providing clear, structured prompts leads to more accurate code suggestions.
2. **Integration with Tools** : Seamless integration with development environments (IDEs) maximises efficiency, allowing real-time feedback and suggestions.
3. **Continuous Learning** : Stay up-to-date with the latest AI tools and features, improving your workflow and expanding the services you offer.

By leveraging AI-powered coding and debugging tools, you can streamline your development process, reduce errors, and maximise efficiency, ultimately enhancing your earning potential. AI can handle many aspects of coding, from error detection and code generation to performance optimisation, enabling developers to focus on solving complex problems and building innovative solutions.

Chapter 48
Creating Custom AI Writing Prompts

In the age of AI-driven content creation, mastering the art of crafting custom AI writing prompts can be a lucrative skill. These prompts act as instructions that guide AI models like GPT to generate high-quality, relevant content. Whether you're using these prompts for creative writing, marketing copy, or technical content, learning to craft effective ones can significantly boost your productivity and earnings.

Benefits of Custom AI Writing Prompts

1. **Precision and Control** : Custom prompts allow you to direct AI models to generate specific types of content, ensuring the output is aligned with your needs.
2. **Time-Saving** : Well-crafted prompts reduce the need for extensive manual editing by encouraging more accurate initial responses from AI.
3. **Scalability** : With the right prompts, you can scale your content creation process across multiple projects, increasing efficiency and profitability.
4. **Enhanced Creativity** : AI can help generate creative ideas or novel approaches, which is particularly useful for writers, marketers, and content creators.

Practical Tips for Creating Effective AI Writing Prompts

1. **Be Clear and Specific** The more detailed your prompt, the better the AI will understand the type of content you want. Clearly define the topic, format, tone, and any key points you want to include.

- **Example** : Instead of "Write about climate change," try "Write a 300-word article explaining how rising global temperatures affect polar bear habitats."

2. **Define Structure and Length** If you want the AI to produce content with a specific structure or length, make sure you specify this in the prompt.

   - **Example** : "Write a 500-word blog post in three paragraphs discussing the benefits of meditation for stress relief."

3. **Provide Context** Adding background information or context helps the AI generate content that is more relevant and informed.

   - **Example** : "Write a product description for a smartwatch targeted at fitness enthusiasts, highlighting the heart rate monitor and waterproof features."

4. **Use Examples** If you want the AI to follow a particular style or tone, provide examples within your prompt to guide the response.

- **Example** : "Write an email marketing campaign in a friendly tone like this: 'Hey there! We've got something exciting for you…'"

5. **Incorporate Keywords for SEO** For SEO content, include keywords in the prompt to ensure the AI includes them in the generated content. This increases the likelihood of ranking higher in search engine results.

   - **Example** : "Write a 700-word article on 'vegan meal prep' including the keywords 'plant-based recipes,' 'easy meal prep,' and 'healthy vegan meals.'"

6. **Iterate and Optimise** Don't expect the first prompt to generate the perfect output. Experiment with different versions of the prompt, adjusting phrasing and details to improve the quality of the content.

   - **Example** : Start with "Write a social media post about summer fashion trends," then refine it to "Write a 100-word Instagram post in an upbeat, conversational tone about the latest summer fashion trends, including hashtags #SummerStyle and #FashionTrends."

Examples of Custom AI Writing Prompts

1. **Creative Writing**

   - "Write a short story (300-500 words) set in a futuristic world where humans and robots live in harmony, but an unexpected event changes everything."

2. **Technical Content**

   - "Write a step-by-step guide explaining how to install WordPress on a self-hosted server for beginners, using simple language."

3. **Marketing Copy**

   - "Create a persuasive product description for a luxury skincare brand's new anti-ageing cream, focusing on its natural ingredients and rejuvenating properties."

4. **Educational Content**

- "Write a 500-word article on the history of the Industrial Revolution for a middle school audience, using clear and simple language."

5. **Social Media**

- "Generate a fun, engaging tweet promoting an eco-friendly water bottle, encouraging people to switch from plastic bottles, with hashtags #SustainableLiving and #EcoFriendly."

Resources for Enhancing Prompt Crafting Skills

- **OpenAI's API Documentation** : Explore detailed guides and best practices for using GPT-based models to craft effective prompts.
- **Prompt Engineering Communities** : Join forums and communities where people

share their most successful prompts, like OpenAI's Discord or Reddit's AI communities.

- **AI Tools and Extensions** : Utilise tools like AI Dungeon or ChatGPT Playground to experiment with prompt crafting in real time.

Maximising Your Earning Potential with Custom AI Writing Prompts

1. **Offer Custom Content Creation Services** Market your expertise in crafting AI prompts for clients who need high-quality, scalable content. Businesses, marketers, and writers can benefit from tailored content for blogs, social media, or email marketing.

   - **Example** : Offer prompt-based content services where clients provide a brief, and you create the ideal prompts for generating articles, product descriptions, or email copy.

2. **Develop AI-Optimised Writing Templates** Create reusable prompt templates for different industries or types of content (e.g., real estate listings, travel blogs, e-

commerce descriptions). You can sell these as digital products or offer them as part of a content package.

- **Example** : Develop and sell an ebook or toolkit filled with pre-made prompts for common content requests like SEO articles or product reviews.

3. **AI Prompt Consulting** Offer consulting services where you help businesses or individuals optimise their use of AI tools by teaching them how to craft more effective prompts.

- **Example** : Set up workshops or one-on-one consultations to teach clients how to use GPT-powered tools for efficient content creation, improving their workflow and output.

4. **Monetise Custom Prompts in Niche Markets** Niche industries often require specialised content. By mastering prompts tailored to specific fields (e.g., legal writing, technical manuals, medical content), you can tap into high-demand, high-paying markets.

- **Example** : Work with legal firms to create AI-driven summaries of case studies or contracts using carefully crafted prompts.

Success Factors in Creating Custom AI Writing Prompts

1. **Understanding the AI's Capabilities** : Knowing what the AI can and cannot do is key to crafting effective prompts. Test the AI's limits and refine your prompts accordingly.
2. **Tailoring to Audience Needs** : Always consider the end audience when crafting prompts. Adjust the tone, complexity, and structure of the prompts based on the content's intended reader.
3. **Constant Learning and Experimentation** : Continuously refine your prompts based on AI output and client feedback. Stay updated on the latest AI tools and capabilities to maintain a competitive edge.

Conclusion

Creating custom AI writing prompts is a valuable skill that can significantly enhance the quality of content generated by AI tools. By mastering prompt engineering, you can offer premium content creation services, boost productivity, and maximise your earning potential. Experiment with different styles, contexts, and specifications in your prompts to consistently deliver content that meets the highest standards. With the right approach, you can use AI as a powerful partner in your content creation journey.

Chapter 49
Providing Personal Branding Content

In today's digital world, personal branding is essential for anyone looking to stand out, whether they are entrepreneurs, influencers, or professionals. Offering personal branding content creation services can be highly profitable. By leveraging AI, you can produce high-quality, engaging content that showcases your clients' unique strengths, skills, and personality, helping them to build a powerful online presence.

Benefits of Providing Personal Branding Content

1. **Customisation and Personalisation** : Tailored content allows individuals to highlight their unique attributes, experiences, and values, helping them to stand out in a competitive space.
2. **Consistency Across Platforms** : Personal branding content ensures a cohesive message across multiple channels, including social media, blogs, and websites.
3. **Increased Engagement** : Thoughtful, well-constructed content can significantly increase audience engagement, helping to build a loyal following.
4. **Career Advancement** : For professionals, strong personal branding can lead to better job opportunities, partnerships, or recognition within their industry.

Practical Tips for Creating Personal Branding Content

1. **Define the Brand's Core Message** Before creating content, understand the individual's brand identity. What are their core values?

What do they stand for? Ensure this message is consistent across all content.

- **Example** : A professional's brand may focus on innovation, leadership, or expertise in a specific field, such as digital marketing or tech.

2. **Develop a Content Strategy** Create a detailed content plan that outlines key topics, target audiences, and the platforms where the content will be distributed.

- **Example** : For a thought leader in finance, the strategy may include LinkedIn articles, Twitter threads, and informative blog posts on industry trends.

3. **Use Storytelling Techniques** Personal branding content should incorporate storytelling to humanise the brand and make it more relatable. Stories about overcoming challenges, key career moments, or personal experiences can make the brand more compelling.

- **Example** : Share a narrative of how a client transitioned from corporate to entrepreneurship, detailing the lessons learned along the way.

4. **Consistency in Tone and Style** Establish a clear voice and tone for the content. Whether it's formal, casual, or motivational, consistency across all platforms is key to building a recognisable personal brand.

   - **Example** : A fitness coach may adopt an energetic, positive tone in all content, while a lawyer might use a more professional, authoritative voice.

5. **Optimise for SEO** Ensure that blog posts, articles, and website content are optimised for search engines. Use relevant keywords that will help the content rank higher, making it easier for potential clients or followers to discover the brand.

   - **Example** : For a marketing consultant, keywords such as "digital marketing strategy," "SEO tips," and "social media trends" can be integrated into blog posts and profiles.

6. **Leverage AI for Content Generation** Use AI tools like GPT to create high-quality content quickly. AI can help generate blog posts, social media captions, and email newsletters efficiently, allowing you to scale your services.

- **Example** : Use GPT to draft LinkedIn posts summarising key industry trends, which can then be refined for a personal touch.

Examples of Personal Branding Content

1. **Social Media Posts**
Regular, engaging posts on platforms like LinkedIn, Twitter, and Instagram that align with the individual's brand message.

- **Example** : "As a digital nomad, staying productive while travelling can be a challenge. Here are my top three tips for managing work-life balance on the road."

2. **Blog Articles**
   In-depth articles that showcase expertise in a particular field, offering valuable insights or advice to the audience.

   - **Example** : "5 Digital Marketing Trends Every Entrepreneur Should Know in 2024."

3. **Profile Bios**
   Well-crafted bios for social media profiles, websites, or portfolios that succinctly summarise an individual's experience, achievements, and goals.

   - **Example** : "Marketing strategist with 10+ years of experience helping small businesses grow through data-driven campaigns."

4. **Personal Website Content**
   A personal website serves as a central hub for an individual's brand, so the content should reflect their professional journey, skills, and future goals.

- **Example** : Write a compelling 'About Me' section that details key career milestones and personal aspirations.

5. **Video Scripts**
   As video content continues to rise in popularity, writing scripts for personal branding videos, whether for YouTube or social media, can be highly impactful.

   - **Example** : A 60-second video script introducing an entrepreneur's new online course, highlighting the value and benefits to potential students.

Resources for Crafting Personal Branding Content

- **Canva** : Create visually appealing personal branding materials such as social media posts or blog headers.
- **Grammarly** : Use for grammar and style checks to ensure all content is polished and professional.
- **AI Tools** : Platforms like GPT-4 or Jasper.ai to help generate initial drafts or content ideas.

- **HubSpot** : Provides insights and templates for personal branding strategies and content planning.
- **LinkedIn Learning** : Courses on personal branding, content marketing, and storytelling can enhance your ability to deliver top-notch content for clients.

Maximising Your Earning Potential

1. **Offer Personal Branding Packages**
   Provide clients with complete branding solutions, including social media content, blog posts, and website copy. These packages can be customised based on the client's needs and industry.

   - **Example** : Offer a "Branding Starter Kit" that includes a personalised bio, social media profile updates, and three blog posts tailored to the client's niche.

2. **Create DIY Resources** Develop ebooks or guides on how to build a personal brand, which can be sold as digital products. These resources could include prompt templates, branding tips, or content strategies.

- **Example** : Write an ebook on "Building Your Personal Brand on LinkedIn: A Step-by-Step Guide," which could be marketed to professionals or job seekers.

3. **Consulting Services** Offer one-on-one coaching or workshops to help individuals define and build their personal brand. You can advise them on content creation, social media strategies, and how to engage their audience effectively.

   - **Example** : Host virtual workshops for professionals looking to enhance their online presence, offering personalised content plans and feedback.

4. **Niche Specialisation** Focus on a particular niche (e.g., tech entrepreneurs, fitness influencers, or corporate leaders) to provide specialised personal branding services. By becoming an expert in a niche, you can charge premium prices for your tailored expertise.

   - **Example** : Work exclusively with startup founders to create compelling

brand narratives that attract investors
and partners.

Conclusion

Providing personal branding content is a highly
valuable service that can help individuals stand
out in a crowded digital space. By developing
clear strategies, crafting personalised content,
and leveraging AI tools for efficiency, you can
help your clients achieve their branding goals
while maximising your own earning potential.
Offering tailored content packages, consulting
services, and niche expertise can further enhance
the value of your services, making personal
branding content creation a profitable endeavour.

Chapter 50
Hosting AI-Powered Writing Workshops

AI-powered writing workshops can be an
excellent way to monetise your expertise while
helping others unlock the power of AI tools, such
as GPT, to enhance their writing skills. These
workshops can cater to different audiences, from
professional writers and marketers to students

and entrepreneurs looking to streamline their content creation process. By offering hands-on, practical sessions, you can teach participants how to use AI to generate content more efficiently, creatively, and effectively.

Benefits of Hosting AI-Powered Writing Workshops

1. **Widespread Appeal** : AI writing tools can be used across various industries, allowing you to attract a diverse audience, including content creators, marketers, students, and business owners.
2. **High Demand for Writing Tools** : As AI becomes more integrated into workflows, more people are seeking to understand how to use it for writing purposes, offering you an opportunity to meet this demand.
3. **Potential for Recurring Revenue** : Workshops can be hosted regularly, either in person or online, and recorded sessions can be sold as evergreen content, generating passive income.

Practical Tips for Hosting AI-Powered Writing Workshops

1. **Identify Your Target Audience** Before planning your workshop, define the specific group you want to cater to, such as bloggers, copywriters, or entrepreneurs. Understanding your audience will help you tailor the content and examples to their needs.

   - **Example** : A workshop for copywriters might focus on using AI to generate ad copy, while one for bloggers could highlight AI's role in brainstorming ideas and improving SEO.

2. **Create a Detailed Workshop Plan** Develop a step-by-step agenda for your workshop, covering all the basics of AI-assisted writing and gradually progressing to advanced techniques. Include demonstrations, live practice sessions, and time for Q&A.

   - **Example** : Start with an introduction to AI-powered writing tools, followed by practical exercises on using GPT to generate blog posts, product descriptions, and email campaigns.

3. **Focus on Real-World Applications** Show participants how AI writing tools can be applied in practical scenarios to improve efficiency and creativity. Tailor examples to their specific industries and writing needs.

   - **Example** : For marketers, demonstrate how to use AI to draft compelling email subject lines, generate social media captions, or refine SEO-focused blog posts.

4. **Provide Hands-On Experience** Encourage attendees to bring their own projects, such as articles or sales copy, to work on during the session. This practical element will allow them to see how AI can be integrated into their current writing workflow.

   - **Example** : Guide participants through the process of using GPT to rewrite sections of their blog post, refining language and improving readability.

5. **Use AI Writing Tools in the Workshop**
   Demonstrate AI-powered platforms like GPT-4, Jasper.ai, or Sudowrite during the session. Show attendees how to use the tools effectively, offering tips for fine-tuning the outputs.

   - **Example** : Show participants how to input clear, concise prompts to get the best results from GPT, and how to revise AI-generated content to ensure quality and originality.

6. **Offer Follow-Up Resources** Provide attendees with access to resources such as templates, prompt examples, and guides on how to use AI in their writing. These materials will add value to the workshop and help participants continue learning after the session ends.

   - **Example** : Share a PDF guide with top prompts for different types of content, such as blog posts, social media updates, and product descriptions.

Examples of AI-Powered Writing Workshop Topics

1. **AI in Content Marketing**
   Teach marketers how to use AI to generate SEO-optimised blog posts, email newsletters, and social media content.

   - **Example** : Show how to use AI tools to create content that ranks highly on Google and engages readers.

2. **AI for Creative Writers**
   Focus on how novelists, poets, and scriptwriters can use AI to spark new ideas, develop plots, and overcome writer's block.

   - **Example** : Demonstrate how AI can help with brainstorming character backstories or drafting scene outlines for novels.

3. **Using AI for Business Writing**
   Help business professionals use AI tools to draft reports, proposals, and presentations more efficiently.

- **Example** : Show how AI can generate the first draft of a business proposal, which can then be edited and refined.

4. **AI-Powered Resume and Cover Letter Writing**
   Assist job seekers in using AI to craft compelling resumes and cover letters that stand out to potential employers.

   - **Example** : Guide attendees through the process of inputting their job history and skills into an AI tool to produce tailored cover letters.

Maximising Your Earning Potential

1. **Charge for Workshop Attendance** Offer live or recorded workshops as paid sessions. You can create different pricing tiers depending on the depth of the content or the level of personal feedback and interaction offered.

   - **Example** : Charge a premium for small, hands-on workshops that include personal feedback on participants' AI-generated writing.

2. **Create Recorded Workshop Courses** Record your live workshops and sell them as on-demand courses. These can be hosted on platforms like Udemy, Teachable, or your own website, generating passive income.

   - **Example** : Create a series of pre-recorded videos demonstrating how to use AI tools for specific writing tasks, such as crafting blog posts, emails, or product descriptions.

3. **Offer Private Workshops or Consultations** For clients or companies looking for more personalised advice, offer one-on-one coaching sessions or private workshops. These can focus on the unique needs of their business or writing goals.

   - **Example** : Run bespoke workshops for marketing agencies on how to implement AI for scaling content production.

4. **Bundle Workshops with Additional Resources** Increase the perceived value of your workshops by including bonus resources such as templates, checklists, and e-books that complement the learning experience.

   - **Example** : Include an AI writing prompt guide or content creation checklist as a bonus with every workshop purchase.

5. **Host Free Webinars to Build a Following** Offer a free introductory webinar on AI-powered writing to build an audience. You can then promote your paid workshops to these participants and offer them a discount as an incentive.

   - **Example** : Run a free, 30-minute webinar on "AI-Powered Writing Tips for Beginners" and follow it up with a paid, in-depth workshop.

Resources for Hosting AI-Powered Writing Workshops

- **Zoom or Google Meet** : For hosting online workshops with live demonstrations and participant interaction.
- **Notion or Google Docs** : Share workshop materials such as prompts, templates, and example content with attendees.
- **Udemy or Teachable** : Platforms where you can create and sell recorded versions of your workshops as online courses.
- **AI Tools** : GPT-4, Jasper.ai, or Sudowrite for practical demonstrations during the workshops.

Conclusion

Hosting AI-powered writing workshops is an excellent opportunity to share your expertise, educate others, and generate a steady income. By carefully targeting your audience, offering practical, hands-on training, and providing valuable follow-up resources, you can build a successful business that leverages the growing demand for AI in content creation. Expanding into recorded courses, private consultations, and downloadable materials can further increase your earnings while helping others harness the power of AI to enhance their writing.